EDUCATION
and the
SOUL

EDUCATION and the SOUL

TOWARD A SPIRITUAL CURRICULUM

John P. Miller

with a foreword by Thomas Moore

State University of New York Press

Published by
State University of New York Press, Albany

© 2000 State University of New York

For information, address State University of New York Press
State University Plaza, Albany, New York 12246

Production by Dana Foote
Marketing by Dana Yanulavich

Thanks to the following for their assistance:
 Interlink Trust, 64 Archery Steps, St. Georges Fields, London W2 2YF, for
material from *Presenting the Case for Meditation in Primary and Secondary
Schools,* by Gina Levete; and to Paul Moss for quotations from that
publication.
 Institute for Integrative Learning and Teaching, 1514 North Blair, Royal
Oak MI 48067 for material from *Mindsight,* by Beverly-Colleene with Anne
Bruetsch.
 Marina Quattrocchi for material from the dreamwork section of her
doctoral thesis at the Ontario Institute for Studies in Education.
 Bernie Neville for quotations from his book *Educating Psyche.*
 Caddo Gap Press for quotations from *School with Forest and Meadow,* by
Ikue Tezuka.
 Floyd Robinson for the earth activities in chapter 6.
 Peter Corcoran for the creed of the Soule School.

Library of Congress Cataloging-in-Publication Data
Miller, John P., 1943–
    Education and the soul : toward a spiritual curriculum / John P.
 Miller ; with a foreword by Thomas Moore.
        p.   cm.
    Includes bibliographical references and index.
    ISBN 0–7914–4341–8 (hc : alk. paper). — ISBN 0–7914–4342–6
 (pbk. : alk. paper)
    1. Moral education. 2. Spiritual formation. 3. Education
 Curricula. 4. Soul. I. Title.
 LC268.M52   1999
 370.11′4—dc21   99–31605
                                                        CIP

10   9   8   7   6   5   4   3   2

Contents

Foreword

The Soul as Educator

What does it mean to be an educated person? Is it someone who knows what the society believes is important information? Is it someone who has sufficient skill to make a good living? Is it someone who has read and traveled widely? Or could we consider educated the person who is free of paranoia and narcissism, who has sufficient tranquility of heart to be compassionate and can make a real contribution to the community?

Most books and essays on education that I have read begin with the word. "Education," they remind us, means to lead out. It's strange that though the word has to do with bringing forth what is present, our usual practice is to stuff what we consider valuable into a mind we consider empty. This approach should logically be called *in*duction—forcing in, not leading out.

If we imagined that a child is a complete human being, born with the fullness of spirit and talent, simply in need of unfolding, then we might be able to educate. We could lead forth all that fresh human stuff for our benefit and for the fulfillment of the child. The three letters *duc* in education are from the same root as the word duke, a leader. Educators are leaders because, like a pied piper, they entice all that latent stuff out into the world, where it enriches us all.

The stuff that comes with the child, however, is not science, logic, or mechanical skill. It is soul stuff. It is imagination, heart, and creativity. It is spirit and vision. An educated person is someone whose innate being has been led out, enticed and appreciated. Education is not at all the same as teaching. It is accomplished by love and faith in the very soul of the child who stands before us crammed with unmanifested talent.

The soul of some children will be revealed in mathematics, some in art, some in politics. When we educate for the soul, we must reflect on our own values and expectation and then ask ourselves:

Are we making little replicas of ourselves, or are we leading forth what was planted in eternity? Are we cramming what we judge appropriate into the child, or are we loving this new stuff we glimpse in the fresh being in our charge?

Real education takes place in an envelope. We can be surrounded by the mist of the soul's mystery, not knowing exactly what we are doing or where we are going. The soul asks faith, not control. It is not anxious about the future but enjoys what is emerging in the present.

Once we shift from mind to soul, our teaching will change radically. It will follow the lines developed so imaginatively and comprehensively by Jack Miller in these pages. It will ask the land to be a teacher. Thoreau said that we all need to be instructed by the plants and flowers around us. It will be a place of abundant imagination, where images can flow and be painted and sculpted without restriction and exploitation. It will embrace the craving for spirit that offers vision and the most grounding kind of security.

This soul education is not expected ever to be perfect. One of the joys of working with the soul is that ignorance is not an evil and mistakes are a path toward beauty. In this kind of education, we cherish the individual child and care not at all about conformity. We are not anxious about mental development, because what makes a human being a person is the heart, not the head.

As Jack Miller says, we also have to take the teacher's soul into consideration. It, too, is in the envelope. And wherever soul is at work, its means of creativity is love. Not sentimental love, but strong, robust engagement of the heart. We learn about a thing from our love for it. Without felt love, learning becomes a sado-masochistic endeavor in which everyone suffers needlessly. In real education, suffering means being affected, not feeling pain.

To introduce the soul into education, therefore, is a radical proposal, and yet it is a gentle enterprise. But we all know that gentleness always requires deep-seated strength and security. Only the insecure become aggressive. Soul education requires imagination, not force.

I can't imagine anything more important to our society than to bring soul back into education. In that spirit I support Jack Miller's leadership as he plays the role of duke, leading us all into the world where the genius in each of us may take root and find joyful manifestation.

—Thomas Moore

Acknowledgments

Several people helped contribute to the soul of this book. Linda Rogers, my friend and colleague edited an initial draft. She also suggested certain ideas and quotations that I have included in this work.

Another friend and colleague, Floyd Robinson, also read and commented on an earlier draft of this book. I have been able to include some of his suggestions in the final draft and appreciated very much his interest in this book.

Special thanks also to Thomas Moore for writing such a thoughtful foreword.

I also appreciated the feedback from two other colleagues: David Marshak and Jeffrey Kane whose feedback I also have attempted to include in the revisions of this book.

Priscilla Ross and Jennie Doling from State University of New York Press have also been very helpful in the editing of this book. I have especially appreciated that the careful review process that they have conducted that has helped improve the manuscript.

I would like to thank my students at the Ontario Institute for Studies in Education at the University of Toronto and also the students at Kobe Shinwa Women's University in Japan with whom I have had a chance to discuss many of the ideas in this book. Their souls have inspired me a great deal in my life and work.

Finally, I thank Midori Sakurai with whom I have shared many of these ideas in this book and whose soul continues to nourish my own soul.

Part I

Exploring Soul

1

Education and the Soul

In the last few years we have witnessed an increasing interest in matters of spirituality. Some argue that we are in a spiritual renaissance:

> There is a spiritual renaissance sweeping the world. . . . It is a revolution in the way we think. (Williamson 1994, p.3)

People, of course, can take issue with this claim but one piece of evidence that supports Williamson's claim is that interest around the concept of soul. Through the work of Thomas Moore (1992, 1994) and others, the word "soul" has found its way into various domains including business (Secretan 1996) and politics (Wallis 1994). I think this interest can be explained because people feel that something is "missing" in their lives. People who have achieved a degree of material affluence often end up asking the question: "Is that all?"

Many people detect an emptiness in society and in their own lives. In attempting to find the source of this emptiness Moore and others have asserted that part of the problem comes from a lack of soul. Without soul, our society seems to lack a basic vitality or energy. Except for the energy in consuming and producing, the way many people feel is summed up by a cover of *Newsweek* (March 6, 1995) that showed a man's tired face with the title: "Exhausted." People on the streets, subways, in the shopping malls often look exhausted, disgruntled, or angry. As a result, people seek fulfillment, or escape, in alcohol, drugs, work, and a variety of other addictions.

The pace of life itself is soulless. We all seem in a mad rush to acquire and consume, with little time for simple pleasures. We are not satisfied with just feeling fresh air on our cheeks or watching children at play. Children too feel the pressure. David Elkind

(1981) has written about the *Hurried Child*. Children can find their lives programmed with not only school but other activities that their parents feel are essential to their development. Children are driven from one event to another as they become part of their parents' hectic schedule. Elkind describes some of the other characteristics of the hurried child:

> Hurried children are forced to take on the physical, psychological and social trappings of adulthood before they are prepared to deal with them. We dress our children in miniature adult costumes (often with designer labels), we expose them to gratuitous sex and violence, and we expect them to cope with an increasingly bewildering social environment—divorce, single parenthood, homosexuality. Through all of these pressures the child senses that it is important for him or her to cope without admitting the confusion and pain that accompany such changes. (p. xii)

Education has become part of this scenario. We are told constantly that the purpose of schooling is to prepare our children to compete in a global economy. There is rarely any mention of a broader vision of education that includes a focus on the whole person. The emphasis is primarily economic. "Education" in many cases has become a series of tests and hurdles rather than focusing on learning. Alfie Kohn (1993) has found that the more we emphasize tests and rewards the less children learn. As a result, schooling can become a grim pastime where children feel a variety of academic and social pressures. The results of all this are summarized by Robert Sardello (1992):

> Education instead has become an institution whose purpose in the modern world is not to make culture, not to serve the living cosmos, but to harness humankind to the dead forces of materialism. Education as we know it, from preschool through graduate school, damages the soul. (p. 50)

We can reclaim our souls. Instead of denying and oppressing the soul we can learn to let the soul manifest itself in the world. Instead of confining the soul, we can learn to celebrate soul. By reclaiming soul, we find that the classroom, or any educational encounter, takes on a new vitality and purpose. Students and teachers no longer go through the motions, but instead feel alive and nourished in what they do.

This book is about how we can bring soul into our classrooms and schools. It is also about how we as teachers and administrators can nurture our own souls. A basic assumption of this book is that the more we are able to nourish our own souls the more our teaching or work will be reenergized and revitalized. Bringing soul into education is not to deny the need to teach skills to our students so that they can be productive citizens. Soulful education is also education with high expectations. However, soulful learning seeks to restore a balance between our outer and inner lives.

GLOBAL CONTEXT

I think it is important to link the need for soulful education with other changes that are taking place on the planet. As noted earlier Williamson has called this a "spiritual renaissance"; I prefer the term "global awakening." People in different countries and in different domains are awakening to a sense of the sacred and to the interconnectedness of life.

The ecology movement and concern for the environment has played a major role in this process. Recent global conferences on the environment demonstrate the desire of people to prevent the further degradation of the planet and the biosphere. The environmental movement has shown us how everything is so deeply interconnected. We can no longer live under the delusion that we can separate the economy from the environment. For centuries humans felt that they could do almost anything and no problems would result. Now we know that any changes we introduce into our lives will have some effect and that we must try to take these changes into account if we want to protect the soil, the air, and the water that support all life. Ecology as well as the traditions of indigenous people has drawn the metaphor of the web to portray this interconnectedness. If we can see ourselves as part of the web of life there is less chance that we will tear this web apart.

This awakening to the interdependence has also encouraged us not only to look at our actions but our thoughts and inner life as well. Many see the source of ecological problems arising from an inner poverty. Al Gore (1992) has written:

> The more deeply I search for the roots of the global environmental crisis, the more I am convinced that it is an outer manifestation of an inner crisis that is, for lack of a better word, spiritual. . . . I have come to believe in the value of a kind of inner ecology that relies on the same principles of balance and holism that characterize a healthy environment. (pp. 12, 367)

Gore and others have made the connection then between soul and the problems that confront our world. Simply put, if our beings our filled with greed, aversion and anger, then the world around us will reflect that inner state. Of course, there is an interaction between our inner and outer worlds but lack of attention to the inner world tends to exacerbate the problems we face. The following words of the Buddhist tradition I think are appropriate here:

> The thought manifests as the word,
> The word manifests as the deed,
> The deed develops into habit,
> And the habit hardens into character.
> So watch the thought
> And its ways with care,
> And let it spring from love
> Born out of respect for all beings. (source unknown)

By being more attentive to our inner life, or soul life, we can perhaps help in the process of healing ourselves and the planet.

The environmental ethic of seeing interconnections can be seen also in medicine. Physicians are moving away from seeing the body as a machine and instead are seeing the relationship between mind and body. For example, Redford Williams, an M.D., has made the connection between people's emotional state and heart disease. He has found that particularly damaging to the heart is hostility and anger. People who carry hostility are more prone to heart attacks. In contrast, people who have trusting hearts have a much greater chance to be healthy:

> The trusting heart believes in the basic goodness of humankind, that most people will be fair and kind in relationship with others. Having such beliefs, that trusting heart is slow to anger. Not seeking out evil in others, not expecting the worst of them, the trusting heart expects mainly good from others and, more often than not, finds it. As a result, the trusting heart spends little time feeling resentful, irritable, and angry.
>
> From this it follows that the trusting heart treats others well, with consideration and kindness; the trusting heart almost never wishes or visits harm upon others. Just as our research has shown that the hostile heart is at risk of premature death and disease, it also can reassure that the trusting heart appears protected against these outcomes. (Williams 1989, p. 71)

We can link Williams' research with the Buddhist quote above, which focuses on cultivating compassionate thoughts and also the proverb "As a man thinketh so he is." Our inner state, then, is important to both our own personal well being as well as the health of the planet.

As mentioned earlier, this process of awakening is found in business in the work of Dalla Costa (1995), Covey (1990), Hawley (1993), Secretan (1996), and Senge (1990). Covey, for example, makes the connection between the inner and outer when he cites David O. McKay who said: "The greatest battles of life are fought in the silent chambers of the soul" (cited in Covey 1990, p. 294). Covey adds:

> If you win the battles there, if you settle the issues that inwardly conflict, you feel a sense of peace, a sense of knowing what you're about. And you'll find that the public victories—where you tend to think cooperatively, to promote the welfare and good of other people, and to be genuinely happy for other people's successes—will follow naturally. (p. 294)

Peter Senge (1990) has also written about the changes that are occurring and he believes one of the most important is where people are moving away from fragmenting, or compartmentalizing, problems to where we place our problems in larger contexts so we can see the relationships among the problems we face. This process is called "systems thinking" and is part of a process Senge calls for in developing "learning organizations." He writes about this process in his book *The Fifth Discipline*. At the end of the book he also acknowledges the broader spiritual changes that are occurring when he refers to Rusty Shweikart, the astronaut, and his perceptions of viewing the planet from space. Senge writes:

> At the conclusion of the leadership workshop, someone asked spontaneously, "Rusty, tell us what it was like up there?" He paused for a long time. When he finally spoke, he said only one thing. "It was like seeing a baby about to be born."
> Something new is happening. And it has to do with *it all*—the whole. (p. 371)

There are certain political leaders who are also infusing spirituality in their approach to politics. These leaders include Vaclav Havel, president of the Czech Republic, the Dalai Lama, the spiritual and political leader of the Tibetan people, Nelson Mandela, President of South Africa, and Aung San Suu Kyi, who has become the spiritual and political voice of the Burmese people. Aung San

7

Suu Kyi (1997) when asked about the most important qualities of Burmese culture she wishes to preserve, states: "The Buddhist values of loving-kindness and compassion. A respect for education" (p. 81) Aung San Suu Kyi does not separate spirituality from political life. She says: "I think some people find it embarrassing and impractical to think of the spiritual and political life as one. I do not see them as separate. In democracies there is always a drive to separate the spiritual from the secular, but it is not actually required to separate them" (p. 26). Aung San Suu Kyi meditates every day as part of her spiritual practice. She feels it is important in developing awareness and spiritual strength.

The Dalai Lama (1994) does not see himself a political leader but as simply a monk:

> I am a Buddhist monk, so I try to practice accordingly. When people think this practice is something unique and special and call me a leader of world peace, I feel almost ashamed! . . . It's just that my practice is the peaceful path of kindness, love, compassion, and not harming others. This has become part of me. It is not something for which I have specially volunteered. I am simply a follower of the Buddha. (p. 98)

I believe that Aung San Suu Kyi, the Dalai Lama, Havel, and Mandela are creating a new vision of political leadership that is part of the broader pattern of awakening.

The restoration of soul is part of this pattern of global awakening. People are attempting to infuse soul into every part of our lives in order to revitalize and give deeper meaning and purpose to what we do every day. It is part of a process where we engage the sacred in everyday life. Like Aung San Suu Kyi, more and more people find the barrier between the secular and spiritual to be superficial. Senge (1990, p. 5) and others have discussed how more people are seeing their work as something sacred.

EDUCATION AND SOUL

This book, then, is an attempt to help teachers be part of this broader pattern by bringing soul and the sacred into education. I believe that we can do this in a manner that does not threaten anyone's religious beliefs or traditions but in fact can enhance them. I can speak from personal experience since I teach graduate courses in spirituality in education and holistic education and have had people from every conceivable religious tradition in my classes. I have found that by approaching the spiritual issues and practices in an open and nondogmatic way that we can begin to nourish each other's souls. I discuss this work in chapter 8.

In the next chapter I discuss the nature of the soul in detail. Here I will just give a basic definition that will provide a foundation for the rest of this chapter. *Soul is a deep and vital energy that gives meaning and direction to our lives.*

Why should we infuse our approaches to education with soul?

1. As noted above, the separation between the spiritual and secular is false. To deny spirit is to deny an essential element of our being and thus diminish ourselves and our approach to education. By bringing soul more explicitly into the educational process we can have an education for the *whole person* rather than a fragmented self.
2. By bringing soul into education we can make our classrooms more *vital* and energizing places. Too often the classroom can be a dull and lifeless place. By restoring soul we can bring a basic vitality into the classroom. The last half of this book suggests different ways we might do this.
3. Soulful education can help bring a *balance* to our education between such factors as inner and outer, the rational and intuitive, the qualitative and the quantitative. Our educational systems have tended to emphasize behavior, rational thinking, and the quantitative. It can be argued that our educational system has become out of balance with its overemphasis on technology and accountability. By bringing soul into our classrooms we can develop a harmonious balance between the inner and the outer. Again some ways of restoring balance are discussed in the second part of the book.
4. By acknowledging soul we can face the *"big"* questions of life. These are the questions that most people confront during their lives but are rarely addressed in educational settings. These questions include, what is the nature of reality and truth? What is the purpose of life? Who am I and what is the nature of the human being? These questions can begin when as a child we look up into the cosmos and wonder about the nature of the universe. They continue into adolescence when we can begin to probe more deeply into the purposes of life. These are questions that we come back to throughout our lives, and education

should facilitate this process by examining how science, poetry, religion, and other areas have explored and addressed these questions. A soulful approach to education does not ignore this process and, in fact, allows education to become deeply relevant to the lives of children and adolescents.

In summary a soulful approach to education can help bring vitality and a deeper sense of purpose and meaning to classrooms.

THE BOOK'S FRAMEWORK

This book is divided into two parts. The first part, which includes the first three chapters, explores the nature of the soul. Various conceptions of the soul are examined including my own. The third chapter explores this conception in some detail and in particular discusses how love and work are important to the soul's development.

The second part of the book deals with how we can bring soul into our schools. Chapter 4 discusses a curriculum for the inner life. Specifically, techniques such as meditation, visualization, dreamwork, and autobiography are explored. The chapter is based on the principle stated by Matthew Fox (1994) that we need a massive infusion with regard to our impoverished inner lives.

Chapter 5 explores how the arts can nurture soul. Visual art, music, drama, and creative writing are explored in different contexts. Earth education and how it can support soul are discussed in chapter 6. Some basic principles of earth education are discussed and then several schools and programs are cited as examples of how these approaches can work in practice.

Chapter 7 examines how the school itself has a soul. The work of Secretan (1996) is explored and specifically his conception of the sanctuary, which is an institutional setting that nourishes soul. Ways to enhance the soul of the school are explored. The chapter concludes with several examples of soulful schools.

Perhaps the most important element in soulful learning is the teacher's soul. The teacher's soul must be nourished if the student's soul is to develop. There is nothing that our students desire from us more than our attention, our authentic presence. Only with training and discipline can we reliably offer this to them. In chapter 8 I discuss various ways that we can support this process.

Two qualities that the soulful teacher can usually bring to the classroom are presence and caring. Presence arises from mindfulness where the teacher is capable of listening deeply. In my own work at the Ontario Institute for Studies in Education/University of Toronto, I encourage teachers to bring mindfulness, or moment-to-moment awareness, to the classroom and their interactions with students. Below is a statement by one teacher who is able to bring this awareness to the classrooms.

> As a teacher, I have become more aware of my students and their feelings in the class. Instead of rushing through the day's events I take the time to enjoy our day's experiences and opportune moments. The students have commented that I seem happier. I do tend to laugh more and I think it is because I am more aware, alert and "present," instead of thinking about what I still need to do. (Miller 1995, p. 22)

Closely related to presence is caring. The caring teacher relates the subject to the needs and interests of the students. Nel Noddings (1984) who has written extensively about caring suggests that when this happens the student "may respond by free, vigorous, and happy immersion in his own projects" (p. 181). When the teacher demonstrates caring, community can develop in the classroom. Marcia Umland, an elementary school teacher, talks about how this can happen:

> When I wanted to spend all that time with those little people in class, I found that the intimacy I had shared with my peers in college in the sixties was carried over into my classroom. I cared about the students and couldn't stand to sit in the teachers' lounge where they were gossiping about their students. . . .
>
> I get exhausted, but not burned out. Sometimes I'm dropping my dream for a day or two, but most days I'm on, and stunned by the kids. Lately I've realized that in setting up in a classroom at last I've given myself permission to form a society I'd like to live in. (Macrorie 1984, pp. 155–61)

In the last chapter I discuss what I consider the basic principles of a soulful approach to education. Finally, I try to deal with the difficult question of how we can have soulful education in our public schools in a nonthreatening way.

I believe that the time has come for soulful learning. We have had enough of machinelike approaches to education that deaden the human spirit. The present trends of outcomes-based education and accountability can drain the vitality from our classrooms. The pressure for quantifying all learning without concern for quality represses the student's soul. Instead, we can learn to bring onto the Earth an education of deep joy where the soul once again learns to sing. Soulful learning nurtures the inner life of the student and connects it to the outer life and the environment. It acknowledges and gives priority to the human spirit rather than simply producing individuals who can "compete in the global economy." Restoring the soul to education is not a new vision. It is a vision articulated by the Greeks and various indigenous people for centuries. It is found in Taoism and the in the teachings of Christ and the Buddha. Why should we aspire to less than our ancestors? Education has lost its way; we need to look to the soul to help recover and remember what Emerson called "our original relationship to the universe."

2

Conceptions of the Soul

What is the soul? For centuries human beings have attempted to describe the nature of the soul. It has proven to be an elusive yet compelling task generating a never ending outpouring of opinion from scholarly works to the popular press, even in this materialistic age. In this chapter I explore various conceptions of the soul from various religious and philosophic traditions.

RELIGIOUS VIEWS OF THE SOUL

Hinduism

The Hindu word for the individual soul is *jiva*. This jiva begins within the simplest forms of life and gradually grows and enters into more complex forms as it develops. This movement from one life form to another is called "transmigration of the soul." According to Huston Smith (1986), this progression is automatic until the soul incarnates in a human body (p. 100). However, when the soul enters the human body, it becomes self-conscious and thus becomes responsible for its own development.

The concept of karma is important here. Karma basically refers to the moral law of cause and effect. In the Bible we also find this concept—"as a man sows, so shall he reap." In most forms of Christianity, however, there is offered the concept of grace through Christ to help us transcend our karma, but Hinduism concedes no escape from karma. Smith comments: "Each act he directs upon the world has its equal and opposite reaction on himself. Each thought and deed delivers an unseen chisel blow toward the sculpturing of his destiny" (p. 101).

According to Hindu belief, when the soul first incarnates in the human body, it pursues sensual delights. In a series of lifetimes, the soul may also focus on gaining power. Eventually, however, the soul grows tired of these attachments and begins to seek freedom. In Hinduism this can be achieved through various forms of yoga.

Yoga, which means union, allows the person to connect to his or her atman, or divine essence. Some types of yoga like Hatha Yoga (physical positions) are well known in the West. Other types of yoga such as Bhakti Yoga (devotional yoga) would not be recognized as yoga by most Westerners. But whatever path is chosen by the Hindu devotee, by realizing atman, the person is joined with the universal spirit-soul, Brahman. Through this union freedom and wholeness are realized.

Buddhism

The Buddha denied the existence of a separate soul that has inherent substance. However, he did acknowledge karma and the concept of reincarnation. What then is reincarnated each lifetime? The image that the Buddha used was the passage of a flame from one candle to another candle. So what moves from one body to another is not a substance but an energy or process with certain tendencies. These tendencies are the result of the actions and desires of past lifetimes.

Buddha's belief that the soul has no substance is linked with his concept of impermanence. This is the idea that all things arise and pass away. He looked upon life as "a phantom, dew, a bubble" (cited in Smith, p. 174). The soul in Buddhism is not a thing but a process or set of energies that is constantly changing. However, as in Hinduism, we can become free from past karma through the eightfold path:

> Right understanding.
> Right purpose.
> Right speech.
> Right conduct.
> Right livelihood.
> Right effort.
> Right awareness.
> Right concentration, or meditation.

The last two elements are perhaps the most important and of these two, right awareness, or mindfulness, may be the most important element of all where we attempt to be fully awake in everything we do. In chapter 8 I discuss mindfulness in more detail and how it can lead to a more soulful approach to teaching.

Christianity

Within Christianity there have been various conceptions of the soul. A traditional conception of the soul is that the person is born with original sin. In this conception the soul is inherently flawed and can only be saved through Christ. One accepts Christ as personal savior in order to redeem one's soul.

In more mystical conceptions, the view of the soul is not so dark. Here the person is seen as having an inherent divine spark, what Quakers call the "inner light" that one can access through prayer and contemplation. In this conception, we let the Christ within manifest through contemplation. In her book *The Gnostic Gospels* (1979), Elaine Pagels argues that there was a vibrant mystical tradition in early Christianity that was extinguished for political reasons both in the state and within the church. She offers in the introduction to her book the following words from the Gospel of Thomas, evocative of a Zen koan:

> Jesus said, "If you bring forth that which is within you, what you bring forth will save you. If you do not bring forth what is within you, what you do not bring forth will destroy you." (p. xv)

In our times, a leading Christian mystic, Thomas Merton (1959) has explored the soul in his writing. He makes the distinction between the exterior and interior "I."

> But the exterior "I," the "I" of projects, of temporal finalities, the "I" that manipulates objects in order to take possession of them, is alien from the hidden, interior "I" who has no projects and seeks to accomplish nothing, even contemplation. He seeks only to be, and to move (for he is dynamic) according to the secret laws of Being itself, and according to the promptings of a Superior Freedom (that is, of God), rather than to plan and to achieve according to his own desires. (pp. 4–5)

In contrast, the inner self of "I" is characterized by the capacity for the deepest connection with others:

> The inner "I" is certainly the sanctuary of our most personal and individual solitude, and yet paradoxically, it is precisely that which is most solitary and personal in ourselves which is united with the "Thou" who confronts us. We are not capable of union with one another on the deepest level until the inner self in each one of us is sufficiently awakened to confront the inmost sprit of the other. (p. 20)

How can we awaken the inner self? Merton suggests that we can awaken the inner self through contemplation and love. He also argues that the two are closely related:

> In fact, contemplation is man's highest and most essential spiritual activity. It is his most creative and dynamic affirmation of his divine sonship. . . .
>
> Solitude is necessary for spiritual freedom. But once that freedom is acquired, it demands to be put to work in the service of a love in which there is no longer subjection or slavery. Mere withdrawal, without the return to freedom in action, would lead to a static and death-like inertia of the spirit in which the inner self would not awaken at all. (p. 22)

Merton's interior "I" can be linked with soul, which needs both action and love to nurture its development.

Judaism

The mystical thread of Judaism, found in the Kabbalah, also reveals a conception of soul. Hoffman (1980) in discussing the Kabbalah states that within this tradition there are three aspects to the person: (1) *nefesh*, a type of biological energy; (2) the *ruah*, which is another name for the individual's psyche, or soul; and (3) *neshamah*, or the Self, which unites the person with universal divine essence. To bring unity to the person and connection to the divine meditation is suggested as a method for integration. These meditative techniques focus on breathing, repeating letters and phrases, and visualization. Below is one exercise from the Kabbalah called "Unsheathing the Soul."

> Now turn your thoughts to visualizing the Name and its supernal angels, imagining them as if they were human beings standing or sitting around you, with you in the middle like a messenger about to be sent on a royal mission, waiting to hear about it from their lips, either from the king himself or from one of his ministers. Having imagined this vividly, prepare your mind and heart to understand the many things about to be conveyed to you by the letters being contemplated within you. Meditate on them as a whole and in all their detail, like one to whom a parable, a riddle, or a dream is being told, or like one perusing a book of wisdom, pondering a passage beyond his grasp. Interpret what you hear in an uplifting manner, approximating it as best you can. Based on what you understand of it,

evaluate yourself and others. All this will happen after you fling the tablet from your hands and the pen from your fingers, or after they fall by themselves due to the intensity of your thoughts. Realize that the stronger the mental flow, the weaker will become your organs and limbs. Your entire body will begin to tremble violently. You will think that you are about to die because your soul, overjoyed at what she has attained, will depart from your body. Consciously choose death over life, knowing that such death affects only the body and that thereby the soul lives eternally. Then you will know that you are capable of receiving the flow. If you then wish to honor the glorious Name by serving it with the life of body and soul, hide your fact, fear to gaze at God and come no closer, like Moses at the burning bush. Return your spirit to its sheath until another time. Rejoice in what you have, and know that God loves you. (Matt 1995, pp. 103–4)

This exercise is not unlike those found in Eastern spiritual traditions that attempts to bring an awareness of our soul life and connect that soul life to the divine.

Islam

Unlike Christianity, the Islamic faith sees the human as intrinsically good as there is no concept of original sin. Huston Smith (1994) asserts that the closest thing to the Christian concept of original sin is the Islamic notion of forgetting as people can sometimes forget their divine origins. The human soul is seen as having free choice and thus responsibility for its own fate. The Koran states, "whoever gets to himself a sin, gets it solely on his own responsibility" (4:111). Upon death there is the judgment of the soul whereafter the soul goes to heaven or hell. Whether heaven and hell is metaphorical or literal is open to interpretation. The Koran again states "some of the signs are firm and others are figurative" (3:5). In some verses of the Koran the soul seems to judge itself thus assign its own destiny.

Within Islam there is a vibrant mystical tradition known as Sufism. Sufism, like Taoism, purports that the soul and the path to enlightenment are not definable and cannot be expressed through normal language. To attempt to do so is, "to send a kiss by messenger" according to a Sufi phrase cited by Indries Shah (1977) (p. 19). F. E. Peters in his book *Children of Abraham* (1982) states that mysticism was a potent force throughout the early Judeo/Christian/Islamic world and although Mohammed showed little mystical bent, his followers soon developed their own tradition. Some of them adopted a simple woolen cloak a "Suf" (and this is how Sufis got their name). Union with a God, who is defined within Islam as absolutely transcendent, presented philosophical difficulties. Sufis therefore put no faith in philosophy but in charismatic mystical teachers who often spoke in seemingly nonsense verses and stories. Common practices also involved the repetition of lines and words, and practices involving singing and dancing (pp. 137–139).

PHILOSOPHIC VIEWS OF THE SOUL

It has been argued that all Western philosophy has it roots in Aristotle and Plato. One of the elements of the Platonic tradition in Western thought was the soul. In this section I briefly review the Platonic conception of the soul as articulated by Plato, Plotinus, and Emerson.

Plato

Plato presented his view of the soul in several different works including the dialogues and *The Republic*. For Plato, the soul is eternal. The soul is also capable of apprehending truth while sense-knowledge is subject to distortion. The allegory of the cave, which is found in *The Republic,* finds prisoners lost in a world of delusion where their senses deceive them because they only see shadows. When the one prisoner is led out of the cave into the light of the sun (the Good), the prisoner's soul is able to see the true essence of things (the Forms). Since the soul is eternal, much learning is simply recollection, or remembering what the soul already knows and understands. Plato writes in the dialogue *Phaedo,*

> Cebes added: Your favorite doctrine, Socrates [Plato, in effect], that knowledge is simply recollection, if true, also necessarily implies a previous time in which we have learned that which we now recollect. But this would be impossible unless our soul had been in some place before existing in form of man; here then is another proof of the soul's immortality. (Cited in Capaldi, Kelly, and Navia, p. 71)

For Plato education focuses on discovering what the soul already knows. To this end he advocates that we engage in reflection, dialogue, and contemplation to discover the soul and in so doing to gain possession of what the soul knows and desires. Also important

> The decisive importance of education in poetry and music is this: rhythm and harmony sink deep into the recesses of the soul and take the strongest hold there, bringing that grace of body and mind which is only to be found in one who is brought up the right way. . . . Approving all that is lovely, he will welcome it home with a joy into his soul and nourished thereby, grow into a man of a noble-spirit. (p. 58)

James concludes: "The important point . . . is that for Plato, and thus for the Western intellectual tradition that was to follow, music was the key to the human soul, the most potent instrument available to man for enlightenment" (p. 59). Here Plato was influenced by Pythagoras who also felt music could help attune the soul to the divine. Again in chapter 8 I will have more to say about how music can be used in this manner.

Plotinus

Plotinus lived in the third century in Egypt and Rome and is perhaps the most well-known Neoplatonist. He lived in Alexandria, which according to Wilber, was the center of intellectual life in the ancient world.

> Clement and Origen (arguably the two most important of the early Church Fathers) were fellow townsmen of Plotinus. In Alexandria, one had direct access to at least the following teachers or their schools: the Goddess cult of Isis, Mithra worship, Plutarch (eclectic Platonism), the Neo-Pythagoreans, the Orphic-Dionysian mysteries, Apollonius of Tyana, the extraordinary Jewish mystic Philo, Manichaeanism, the all-important Stoics, Numneius, the great African novelist Apuleius, much of the Hermetic writings, the Magi, Brahmanic Hinduism, early Buddhism, and virtually every variety of Gnosticism. (Wilber, p. 333)

Plotinus synthesized much of this thinking into a complete cosmology. For Plotinus, soul was an integral part of this cosmology. The soul is present at all stages of development and gradually expands to take more of the world into itself. Plotinus believed that the individual soul and World Soul eventually integrated and became one. The development of the soul occurs as it contemplates different forms. Wilber cites Plotinus: "All souls are potentially all things. Each of them is characterized by the faculty which it chiefly exercises. The souls, thus contemplating different objects, are and become what they contemplate" (p. 636). By contemplating the

One, the soul becomes the One. This process is not a passive one but involves actively engaging the world and being fully awake as one is in the world.

Emerson

For Emerson, the soul was the central animating source. Geldard (1993) in his analysis of Emerson states:

> In his lexicon, soul, Reason (capitalized to indicate a higher source), instinct, intuition, even certain uses of "thought" formed a description of the organs related to higher knowing and higher consciousness. The position of "soul" in this hierarchy was supreme, the highest attribute of human existence and perception and the connection within the human being to ever higher orders of being namely God or Universal Being. (p. 35)

The most complete description of the soul comes in Emerson's essay on the Oversoul. The individual soul is related to what Emerson called the Oversoul, which is the Unity—what others might call God—in which all things reside. Through the person's soul, the Oversoul flows into the person's being. This is the source of creativity and wisdom or what Emerson (1990) calls "wise silence" (p. 59). Emerson (1990) states:

> When the Universal Soul breathes through a man's intellect, it is genius; when it breathes through his will, it is virtue; when it flows through his affection, it is love. (p. 60)

How important the soul was to Emerson can be seen in his words that the solution to our difficulties is "soul, soul, evermore soul." I will draw more on Emerson in describing my view of the soul at the end of this chapter.

CONTEMPORARY VIEWS OF THE SOUL

Moore

In 1992 Thomas Moore's book *Care of the Soul* appeared and since then his works have been on the bestseller list. This book and its companion, *Soulmates,* have done much to restore soul to modern discourse. Moore's work is based on Marsilio Ficino who lived during the Renaissance and who also wrote about the care of the soul. For Moore:

> "Soul" is not a thing, but a quality or a dimension of experiencing life and ourselves. It has to do with depth, value, relatedness, heart and personal substance. (p. 6)

For Moore, the language of the soul involves images and fleeting impressions whose meanings are not always immediately clear. The soul's goal is not to overcome life's anxieties, but "to *feel existence*" (p. 390). To feel existence the soul does not follow a straight line, but it tends to meander and feel its way. One way that we can feel existence is through love, or what Plato called "divine madness." Moore states that falling in love may have more to do with the soul than with relationship. Through love we seek the beautiful and the eternal. Our plans and tranquillity can be shattered by love, which sweeps us away. Falling in love, then, is one example of how the soul's agenda can take over the normal routine of everyday life. Moore warns that if we attempt to repress the soul, or ignore its longings, these deep desires can come back to haunt us or disturb us in different ways.

Sardello

Robert Sardello has written two books (1992, 1995) on the soul. He is mainly concerned with the relationship between the individual soul and the world soul:

> The circulating force or power I shall call soul, and to make clear that what I am calling soul has little to do with individual life alone, by soul I shall always imply the soul of the world as a way of referring to the inseparable conjunction of individual and world; and further, this is always a conjunction in depth. (1992, p. 15)

I discuss Sardello's work again in the next chapter but I will mention here that he relates his conception of the soul to the mythical figure of Sophia. He states: "Sophia, rhythmic dance of the soul of the world, rainbow of colors and forms, you are the world as a work of art and you demand from us to understand the world artistically rather than intellectually" (p. 27).

The arts that Sardello refers to are concentration, meditation, picture-making, and contemplation. Each of these can be linked with the four earth elements: Earth, Air, Fire, and Water. "With contemplation we enter into the creating powers of elemental earth, contemplation—to move within the temple of the soul of the world. Seen through Sophia, the so-called spiritual disciplines become a way of facing the world with soul" (p. 25).

Hillman

In a recent book (1996) Hillman argues that each person's soul is given a unique daimon. This daimon is like an acorn that leads the soul to a particular destiny, just as the acorn becomes the mighty oak. Hillman argues that each soul has a particular destiny which can and should be discovered during one's life. This destiny can often be seen in terms of a particular image or set of images.

Hillman refers to Plotinus:

> The soul of each of us is given a unique daimon before we are born, and it has selected an image or pattern that we live on earth. This soul-companion, the daimon, guides us here; in the process of arrival, however, we forget all that took place and believe we come empty into this world. The daimon remembers what is in your image and belongs to your pattern, and therefore your daimon is the carrier of your destiny . . . we elected the body, the parents, the place, and the circumstances that suited the soul and that, as the myth says, belong to its necessity. This suggests that the circumstances, including my body and my parents whom I may curse, are my soul's own choice—and I do not understand this because I have forgotten. (p. 8)

Of the modern theorists of the soul, Hillman is the most explicit in discussing the preexistence of the soul and its destiny in human form.

Borysenko

Joan Borysenko (1995) defines soul as "the substance of the universe, knowing itself and growing itself" (p. 45). She believes that nourishment and growth of the soul is the most important purpose of human life. An important feature of soul is the yearning for connection. Because of this yearning Borysenko suggests that "the interconnectedness of our souls makes service for others a natural joy" (p. 47). She suggests that to nourish our souls we need to serve others and also to provide quiet, meditative time for ourselves. She says: "In taking time to open ourselves to our souls, we become better givers to others and are better able to see the love that is the universe" (p. 48). Other ways to nourish the soul that she suggests include being in nature and confronting the difficult issues that life presents us. Like Moore and others Borysenko (1993) believes that the soul at times must grieve and not push away loss and pain.

Wolf

In his book *The Spiritual Universe: How Quantum Physics Proves the Existence of the Soul,* Fred Wolf (1996) defines soul, spirit, and self in the following manner:

> Based on my research, the spirit appears to be virtual vibrations of vacuum energy; the soul turns out to be reflections of those virtual vibrations in time . . . and the self is an illusion arising from reflections of the soul in matter, appearing as the bodily senses as suggested by the Buddha. Hence the three are related but essentially different.
>
> The quantum wave function demonstrates what I mean by a virtual process—one that has an effect even though it is not a result in fact. Thus, this wave function, although never measured, has extremely important physical consequences. The soul arises along this intangible field of probability—as *virtual processes* in the vacuum of space. . . . In other words, the soul is a virtual process and not an entity. (p. 31)

For Wolf the self, or ego, is what we take for our real identity while we tend to lose touch with soul and spirit. Self becomes lost in what we call the "real world" of coming and going and trying to make a living on the material plane. Occasionally we sense our souls when we hear a piece of music, or see a young child, or hear an old woman tell about her life. Wolf makes an extensive review of the literature on the soul but his main arguments come from quantum physics as shown above in his definition. He claims that by listening to soul the human race can become free.

> Humanity needs to listen, until such a time that the voice of the Soul is heard throughout the universe as the only voice of compassion and reason that has ever existed. When this occurs, all humanity will be truly free and the voice of the Soul will sing until the end of time. (p. 320)

My View of Soul

Here I attempt to draw on some of the conceptions outlined above, particularly those of Emerson and Moore, and to clarify my conception of the soul. First, soul connects our ego and spirit. Ego is our socialized sense of self. It gradually evolves during the child's development as he/she defines himself/herself in relation to others (e.g., parents, siblings, friends, schoolmates, teachers, etc.). Ego is our sense of separateness, or the exterior "I," to which Merton refers. Wolf calls it the self. It is how we define ourselves in relation to the rest of the world.

Spirit is the divine essence within. It is the part of us that is beyond time and space. Through spirit, we experience unity with the divine (e.g., Brahman, God, Tao). There is an ascendant and transcendent quality to spirit. Spirit within has been called the atman (Hinduism), Buddha nature, or the Self. Simply put, the spirit calls us to look upward toward the heavens.

Soul connects ego and spirit. There is more of a sense of depth than of ascendance as we tend to look down into our souls. Moore comments: "The soul, always drawn inward, seeks contemplation and the more shadowy, mysterious experience of the underworld" (p. 349). It is through soul that we attempt to link our humanity with our divinity. If there is too much emphasis on spirit then we can lose touch with our humanity and daily life. On the other hand, an overemphasis on human self can let our lives become too narrowly focused on the mundane. Soul connects the human and divine in a mysterious and spontaneous way. The relationship is further pictured in chart 2.1 opposite:

	SPACE	TIME	FOCUS
Ego	Sees Objects as Separate	Objective Time	Control
Soul	Sees Multiplicity and Unity	Subjective Time	Love
Spirit	Sees Unity and Connection	Outside Time	Union

Four Aspects of Soul:

1. Soul is not an entity or thing, but animating energy or process. Consider Emerson's (1990) definition:

> All goes to show that the soul in man is not an organ, but animates and exercises all the organs; is not a function, like the power of memory, of calculation, of comparison, but uses these as hands and feet; is not a faculty, but a light; is not the intellect and the will, but the master of the intellect and the will; is the background of our being, in which they lie,—an immensity not possessed and that cannot be possessed. (p. 174)

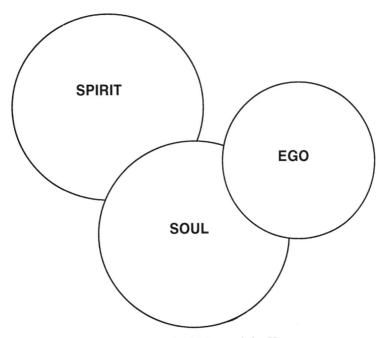

Chart 2.1 The Relationship of the Divine and the Human

As a source of energy we can sometimes feel the soul expand. A beautiful piece of music can make our souls feel expansive; likewise, in a threatening or fearful situation, we can feel our souls contract or shrink. A soulful curriculum would provide a nourishing environment for the soul's expansion and animation.

We can recognize soul in people when we see their eyes light up, when their speech is animated, when their body moves with grace and energy. Sophia Hawthorne saw this quality in Emerson as he walked the streets of Concord:

> It became one of my happiest experiences to pass Emerson upon the street. . . . I realized that he always had something to smile FOR, if not to smile AT; and that a cheerful countenance is heroic. By and by I learned that he always could find something to smile at also; for he tells us, "'The best of all jokes is the sympathetic contemplation of things." (Holmes 1885, 1980, pp. 238–39)

Soulful energy is not just energy, but loving energy. I will have more to say about this shortly.

2. In the soul lie our deepest feelings and longings. When we realize these longings and are able to manifest and work with them we begin to feel deeply fulfilled. In part, we can see life's journey as an attempt to discover and realize these deep longings. One of our deepest longings is to find soulful work. Fox (1994) states:

> Our souls, that is, our awareness and our passions, our ecstasies and our pain are not tidy and small. We, like the rest of the universe, are expanding and are great in size—"magnanimous," Thomas Aquinas calls us, which means literally, "large souled." There is great dignity to our being, great dignity to our work of exploring that inner being and expressing it. (p. 129)

I believe that much of career education is misguided, as often career is viewed as some sort of rational choice. Rationality is part of the process but the soul gradually finds its way in the world and attunes itself to what it feels its life work might be. This often happens through fits and starts as the individual may not find his or her life-fulfilling work until midlife or even later. Thomas Moore (1992) comments:

> We like to think that we have chosen our work, but it could be more accurate to say that our work has found us. Most people can tell fate-filled stories of how they happen to be in their current "occupation." These stories tell how the work came to occupy them, to take residence. Work is a vocation: we are called to it. . . . [F]inding the right work is like discovering your own soul in the world. (pp. 272–73, 279)

3. The soul seeks love. With regard to love the soul seeks union with other souls (e.g., soulmate). This can take the form of romantic love, love of kin, universal love, or love of the divine.

Romantic love in our culture has been trivialized through soap operas and Harlequin romances, or is the target of cynicism. Yet romantic love can teach us a great deal. When we fall in love we see the angelic nature of the beloved. Some say this is a romantic illusion, but perhaps we see the other's true nature, that is, the person's divinity. Through love the soul touches the eternal, the divine. Through wisdom and loving-kindness we can begin to see the angelic nature not only in our beloved but in all beings. We attempt to connect to this inner core of goodness and decency in others.

This is what Nelson Mandela recognized during his twenty-seven years in prison. Although his guards could often be cruel and unfeeling, suddenly he would see an act of kindness that would reveal the more gentle side of the person. Mandela (1994) comments:

> I always knew that deep down in every human heart, there is mercy and generosity. No one is born hating another person because of the color of his skin, or his background, or his religion. People must learn to hate, and if they can learn to hate, they can be taught to love, for love comes more naturally to the human heart than its opposite. Even in the grimmest times in prison, when my comrades and I were pushed to our limits, I would see a glimmer of humanity in one of the guards, perhaps just for a second, but it was enough to reassure me and keep me going. Man's goodness is a flame that can be hidden but never extinguished. (p. 542)

The loving soul attempts to express its joy through music and song. Sardello (1992) comments:

> Soul learning does not consist of the internalization of knowledge, the determination of right meaning, the achievement of accuracy, but is to be found in what sounds right. That the soul sings was understood by the ancient psychology of the soul of the world—the singing of soul was known as the music of the spheres. (p. 63)

The world could use more singing souls. The loving/singing soul feels attunement with the Tao, or the flow of the universe.

Love also motivates us to help make the world a more beautiful place. Theodore Roszak (1992) states that ecologists are motivated by love for the planet and its beauty, rather than by guilt. Action motivated by guilt, no matter how valid, can produce more guilt.

4. The soul dwells in paradox and does not approach life in a linear manner. Although the soul seeks the light of love it also has its shadow side. As Thomas Moore (1992) notes in his book *Care of the Soul,* like Persephone, the soul can be pulled into the underworld in moments of inattention and self-absorption but the "pomegranate seeds of darkness" can help us understand the dark side when we return to spring and the light. We know the phrase the "dark night of the soul" as the soul must deal with loss, grief, and pain, which are an inevitable part of life. If the soul tries to ignore pain, such as the loss of a loved one, then important soul work is being ignored. In North America we are not comfortable with pain and we usually

seek relief in alcohol, TV, movies, and even in the simplistic appeal of fundamentalism. Yet the cost to our souls is enormous as the soul seeks to be in touch with the basic realities of life, which include suffering and death as much as love and joy.

Thus, we must give room for the way of the soul. By listening to the soul we can be sensitive to its ways and needs. One way that we can listen to the soul is through contemplation. Robert Sardello (1995) suggests that soul logic "synthesizes rather than analyzes" (p. xx). According to Sardello, unlike cognitive logic that seeks the right answer, soul logic seeks the healthy answer that serves the whole being. Sardello states: "Illness occurs when something partial is taken to be the whole" (p. xx).

Fragmented approaches to reasoning have been at the root of much of the sickness and alienation in our culture. How can we begin to make informed healthful decisions when our economic system places little value on such things as environmental health, volunteerism, the work of women in the home, and child care? Because we have either refused or been unable to see the interdependence of things, there has been social alienation and environmental decay.

The soul can spend long periods incubating over a problem or conflict. On the surface nothing appears to be happening in relation to the resolution of the problem, but the soul often does not conform to our expectations of time. It has its own timetable. Eventually, however, if allowed to work in its own way, the soul will find a solution or come to peace and let go of its troubles.

Contemplation and soulful knowing are characterized by nonduality. We become that which we contemplate. Consider Emerson's view of contemplation:

> We live on different planes or platforms. There is an external life, which is educated at school, taught to read, write, cipher and trade; taught to grasp all the boy can get, urging him to put himself forward, to make himself useful and agreeable in the world, to ride, run, argue and contend, unfold his talents, shine, conquer and possess.
>
> But the inner life sits at home, and does not learn to do things nor values these feats at all. 'Tis quiet, wise perception. It loves truth, because it is itself real; it loves right, it knows nothing else; but it makes no progress; was as wise in our first memory of it as now; is just the same now in maturity and hereafter in age, as it was in youth. We have grown to manhood and womanhood; we have powers, connection, children, reputations, professions: this makes no account of them all. It lives in the great present; it makes the present great. This

tranquil, well founded, wide-seeing soul is no express-rider, no at-
torney, no magistrate: it lies in the sun and broods on the world.
(Cited in Geldard 1993, p. 172)

Contemplation, which is the soul's main form of learning and
knowing, is hardly ever encouraged in education. Instead we are
taught to find the right answer or develop the right argument. By
ignoring or denying contemplation the soul is also denied. The
soul hides while our minds analyze, memorize, and categorize.

The next chapter deals in more detail with the soul in relation
to love and work since both are so fundamental to the nurturing of
the soul.

3

Love and Work

Freud stated that love and work are essential to a person's well being. Love and work are intimately linked to the soul as they are essential to the soul's expression and destiny.

LOVE

The word "love" is rarely mentioned in educational circles. The word seems out of place in a world of outcomes, accountability, and standardized tests. In a world where "lean and mean" are accepted as desirable qualities, it is not a big jump to see love as a weakness, best kept in check, if not completely repressed. At the very least, our culture doesn't seem comfortable with the word; through popular songs and the media love's meaning has become trivialized. Individuals such as Octavio Paz (1993) argue that the diminishment of love and soul are intertwined.

> The eclipse of the soul has engendered a doubt . . . about what a person really is. . . . A human being, having ceased to be the image and likeness of divinity, now also ceases to be a product of natural evolution and enters the category of industrial production: it is something manufactured. . . . So the expropriation of eroticism and love by the power of money is only one aspect of the twilight of love, the other is the vanishing of love's constitutive element—the person. The two evils complement each other and open up the perspective of a possible future of our society: technological barbarism. (p. 204–5)

In contrast, Paz argues that the ancients saw the universe and planets as a "visible image of perfection" (p. 206). James described this order very well.

Picture to yourself, if you can, a universe in which everything makes sense. A serene order presides over the earth around you, and the heavens above revolve in sublime harmony. Everything you can see and hear and know is an aspect of the ultimate truth: the noble simplicity of a geometric theorem, the predictability of the movements of heavenly bodies, the harmonious beauty of a well-proportioned fugue—all are reflections of the essential perfection of the universe. And here on earth, too, no less than in heavens and in the world of ideas, order prevails; every creature from the oyster to the emperor has its place, preordained and eternal. It is not simply a matter of faith: the best philosophical and scientific minds have proved that it is so. (p. 3)

Within this worldview the soul was also an entity that was related to and governed by the movement of the spheres. The ancients believed that there was a universal energy (*pneuma*) in the cosmos that affected the attractions and repulsions of the planets and that these attractions and repulsions were mirrored in the individual soul, and relations between persons on the earth. Paz claims "the individual soul was part of the universal soul and moved by the forces of attraction and repulsion that move the cosmos" (p. 155).

When this worldview disappeared over the past two or three centuries, it was not replaced by any new sense of order. We are left today with a prevalent random and chaotic view of the world and universe. Paz argues that the present world view of materialism denies the existence of both the soul and love. Inherent in both soul and love is mystery, or the unknowable. Our modern and even post-modern view is that there is very little that is unknowable and what is unknowable is troubling. By contrast, a world view that includes soul and love acknowledges that perhaps the largest part of our experience is unknowable empirically. It is mysterious and wondrous.

The results of a world view where people are without soul is evident. Politically it has aided and abetted holocaust, genocide, and ethnic cleansing. Guards in Hitler's death camps were encouraged to refer to their prisoners as "sticks," "wood," or "fodder." When we see persons as objects without a vital essence then it is easier to exterminate them just as if they were bugs.

The evidence of the loss of soul in love and relationships is also abundant in a world where sexual abuse, violence against women, and what one therapist has termed "intimate terrorism" (Miller 1995) has taken over. Intimate terrorism, as Miller defines it, is the reduction of relationships to a power struggle between competing egos. So many relationships today are defined by this process. Symptomatic of this trend is the popularity of books that purport to teach people the "rules" of the "game" of supposedly loving relationships. When did love become a "game" that could be defined and governed by simplistic "rules"?

Paz argues that love and politics are connected through our conception of the person. He calls on scientists and artists to rediscover "what is most near and everyday: the mystery that each one of us is" (p. 212).

I will explore two aspects of love: love with regard to personal relationships, most specifically the experience of falling in love, and love in a more communal sense and how love joins the individual soul with the world soul.

The Divine Madness

Falling in love is one of the universal human experiences. Like birth, pain, loss, and death, we hear its message across oceans and time. Almost every culture has its tradition of literature, usually poetry, about love and longing. Plato called the experience of falling in love "divine madness." Thomas Moore (1992) suggests love can be viewed more from the perspective of the soul rather than in terms of relationship. He cites the work of a Neoplatonist, Ficino, who argued that "Human love is the desire for union with a beautiful object to make eternity available to mortal life" (Moore, p. 118). Love, or Eros, involves the desire for the beautiful and the eternal. This powerful force does not always work out in terms of a human relationship; yet it is primary to the deepening of the soul. Novalis, the Romantic German poet put it this way: "love was not made for this world" (cited in Moore, p. 118).

When we fall in love we develop an overwhelming feeling for another person. The feeling is so strong that we surrender ourselves to something greater than ourselves. In short, the ego gives up the attempt to control what is happening. Moore suggests that this loss of control "may be highly nutritious for the soul" (p. 137).

Socrates and Plato held the view that love, or what they called Eros, involved the search for wholeness. Referring to Aristophanes and Socrates, Alan Bloom (1993) states, "Eros, in its overwhelming and immoderate demands, is the clearest and most powerful inclination toward lost wholeness" (p. 480).

Love also has a shadow side that is recognition of the inevitability of separation and death. Hegel stated "Lovers can separate from each other only to the degree that they are mortal or when they reflect on the possibility of dying" (cited in Paz, p. 177). Death and separation make any love poignant as the lovers realize that the physical nature of the love cannot be permanent.

Alan Bloom (1993) summarizes some of these ideas:

> The overwhelming attraction we feel toward beautiful objects is central to eroticism, and it follows that eroticism is a painful and needy business and that the beautiful is a perfection outside of the lover. This insistence that the imperfect loves a perfection that does not love is, as I have noted before, in stark contrast to the Romantic ideal of love, which tries to sweeten the one-way character of Eros with the bourgeois myth of reciprocity. This Socratic teaching means from the outset that, in spite of the passion, pleasure, and excitement of Eros, it is something of a hopeless business. (p. 500)

Bloom argues that one of the best examples of an erotic ideal is found in the story of Marcella in *Don Quixote*. Marcella is a beautiful woman who, because of her beauty and her lack of response to her many suitors' overtures, is despised by men. When Don Quixote meets her and inquires about her behavior, she states that nature made her beautiful while making all of her suitors less attractive. She suggests that they should be satisfied with contemplating her beauty rather than possessing her. Bloom comments, "Marcella's speech is perfect Socrates, Plato, and Aristotle in their erotic, cosmological and theological teachings" (p. 501). This longing for the beautiful and the eternal is, in its most active form, "Eros, and Eros is the backbone of the soul" (p. 544). Bloom then concludes: "Man's divination of perfect love or perfect justice is most of all what proves he has a soul" (p. 544).

Thus love, Eros and the soul are intimately connected. When we fall in love we need to ask not so much about how the relationship worked out or didn't work out, but instead turn to questions such as: "Does it bring broader vision? Does it initiate the soul in some way? Does it carry the lover away from earth to an awareness of divine things?" (Moore, p. 118).

Adolescence is a time that often brings the first experience of falling in love. Yet this powerful experience is hardly touched on in the school curriculum, with sometimes disastrous results as young people confront these soul-rending experiences without any preparation or guidance. The broad range of public opinion about how best to educate young people about responsible behavior in their sexual relationships makes this a controversial topic. However, I believe that there is a way that the various conceptions of love and its relationship to soul could be discussed in the secondary school and at the university level. Works such as Plato's *Symposium* and *Don Quixote* could be discussed. Students could begin to see their own intense personal experience from a broader and more insightful perspective. The uncharted country of their strong emotions could find place names and a road map through discussion of literature and philosophy.

Antonio T. de Nicolas (1989) does just this in a philosophy course that he teaches at the university level. One of the activities that he uses is for the students to read and reenact Plato's *Symposium*. Through this experience and others, de Nicolas argues that students learn to imagine in a genuinely creative manner.

Moore (1992) claims that "love releases us into the realm of divine imagination, where the soul is expanded and reminded of its unearthly cravings and needs." He then goes on to state something that is very important. "Love allows a person to see the true angelic nature of another person, the halo, the aureole of divinity" (p. 122).

Here the teacher can connect love to compassion. Love focuses on one person, while compassion is a more universal sentiment that is not exclusive to one person. The student can begin to see that the halo that he or she sees in the beloved is inherent in every human. Through the experience of falling in love, we experience the wonder and mystery that is part of the sacredness of life; through compassion we can see the mystery and sacredness in all living things. The saint, sage or mystic is literally one who has fallen in love with creation. The mystic is not just in love with one person but is intimate with all things.

Connecting to the World Soul

The World Soul has been referred to as Sophia. Sophia is the Goddess found in the Gnostic gospel but from other traditions has been called Isis, Shekinah, Achamoth, Athena, Alchmyia, Spenta, Armatii, and Mary. Sophia is symbolic of the hidden unity that underlies the multiplicity of things. Sardello (1995) comments:

> This totality that all works together does so in relation with all the other planets, the moon, the sun, and the constellations of the zodiac. And there is yet another hiddenness; this unity binds to itself the particularity of every human soul in its individuality. All of this, considered together, is what is indicated by Sophia, Wisdom, the Soul of the World. (pp. 48–49)

Sardello cites a passage from Proverbs to get at the essential quality of Sophia:

> The Lord knew me at the beginning of his ways; before he created anything. I was installed from eternity. When the deeps were not yet in existence, I was already born; when the springs were not flowing with water, before the mountains were set upon their foundations, before the hills, I was born. When he had not yet made the Earth and what is upon it, not the mountains of the surface of the Earth, when he prepared the heavens, I was there. I was there when he measured the deep, when he fixed the clouds above, when he made firm the springs of the deep, when he set a limit to the sea and the waters so that they should not overstep his command, when he laid the foundation of the Earth. (Proverbs 8:22–29)

This conception of Sophia is not unlike the present conception of Gaia. According to Sardello, there are three aspects to Sophia. First, there is heavenly Sophia, or Wisdom, that sees the unity in all things. Second, there is Sophia of the underworld, or chaos. Finally, there is manifest Sophia that is the creation and evolution of the Earth. This last aspect includes Earth in all of its dimensions, including the movement of "light, color, shadow, and the depth of things in their particularities" (p. 54). Sardello suggests that it is through the effort of the individual soul that the three aspects of Sophia can be integrated.

How can this be done? Sardello (1995) refers to the work of Bernard of Clairvaux whose conception of Sophia is represented in Chartres Cathedral, an earth temple of Sophia. According to Bernard, there are three essential qualities of how the individual soul relates to the World Soul. The first quality is what Bernard calls "Reason." Reason, for Bernard, is not the traditional view of rationality, but the ability to have "an inner sense of the inner qualities of outer things as existing in relation with one another; this is the Wisdom of the human soul, the Mother aspect." (p. 51).

The second aspect, which is closely connected to the first quality, is what Bernard calls "imagination." This involves bringing forth images that represent our inner sense of the unity of things. This means that when we plan something, we need to take into account how each element relates to all the other elements. Sardello gives the example of a garden and how "a particular plant relates to all of the plants of the garden, how the garden relates to the rest of the landscape, the landscape to the region, the region to the whole geography, the geography to the rest of the Earth, the rest of the Earth to the cosmos" (p. 51).

Bernard's final element is "memory," which involves seeing the human being as "recollection of the whole of creation." The body is the most evident symbol of this memory. The head represents Reason while the heart is the center of imagination. The body, heart, and head are important in realizing Sophia. All are needed to link the individual soul with the World Soul.

Sardello argues that today's world is one where Sophia is sadly lacking. Our present world is characterized by multiplicity without unity. This, of course, is seen in the fragmentation of life and how we divide our lives into work, vacation, and family. Sardello calls on us to bring soul and love into the world. This is not just an individual act but a communal act where we are conscious of the Earth and the World Soul. One simple way of doing this is a practice suggested by Will Brinton, who heads the Wood End Institute in Maine. Brinton suggests as you walk on the earth see the earth's surface as the skin of a living being. This exercise allows us to see our own consciousness as an expression of Earth's consciousness (Sophia). In short, we are able to see ourselves as intimately linked to the World Soul as expressed in Sophia's words:

> I am Earth in her manifestation as consciousness. I am that quality of consciousness that is the quality of warmth, of feeling. I am not separate from thinking for wherever there is warmth of thinking I am there. I am not separate from willing and doing, for wherever there is the fire of will, I am there. (Cited in Sardello, p. 78)

Another way of seeing ourselves as part of Sophia is to imagine, as Jung did, that the soul is mostly outside the body. In other words, we can see our souls as not localized within ourselves but as an energy field that extends beyond our physical being. This concept is similar to Heidegger's notion of *Dasein*, or "force field." Barrett (1962) comments:

> Existence itself, according to Heidegger, means to stand outside oneself, to be beyond oneself. My Being is not something that takes place inside my skin (or inside an immaterial substance, inside that skin); my Being, rather, is spread over a field or region which is the world of its care and concern. Heidegger's theory of man (and of Being) might be called the Field Theory of Man (or the Field Theory of Matter), provided we take this purely as an analogy. Heidegger would hold that deriving one's philosophic conclusions from the highly abstract theories of physics to be a spurious and inauthentic way to philosophize. But in the way that Einstein took matter to be a

field (a magnetic field, say) in opposition to the Newtonian conception of a body as existing inside its surface boundaries—so Heidegger takes man to be a field or region of Being. (pp. 217–18)

Sardello cites Václav Havel, the president of the Czech republic as someone who articulates this consciousness in his political vision.

It is my profound conviction that we have to release from the sphere of private whim such forces as: a natural, unique and unrepeatable experience of the world, an elementary sense of justice, the ability to see things as others do, a sense of transcendental responsibility, archetypal wisdom, good taste, courage, compassion, and faith in the importance of particular measures that do not aspire to be a universal key to salvation. . . . Soul, individual spirituality, firsthand personal insight into things; the courage to be himself and go the way his conscience points, humility in the face of the mysterious order of Being, confidence in its natural direction and, above all, trust in his own subjectivity as his principal link with the subjectivity of the world—these are qualities that politicians of the future should have. (Cited in Sardello, 1995, p. 79)

I have already suggested that Aung San Suu Kyi, Havel, Nelson Mandela, and the Dalai Lama are examples of political leaders who have been able to connect the individual soul with the World Soul. The inclusive vision that they articulate shows politics can go beyond the power and egotism that characterizes most political activity and move toward a public life based on soul.

Jim Wallis (1994) has described what soulful politics looks like as it contains the following elements:

1. Conversion, or changing the focus of governmental activity supporting the rich and corporations to a primary concern with poverty. He cites the example of the Catholic diocese: before any decision is made, the first question asked is "how will this decision affect the poor?" He suggests that all public policy questions should begin with this question.
2. Compassion—where we no longer divide people into us and them.
3. Community, or the movement toward "decentralization, community-based economies, ecological planning, appropriate technology, sustainable, organic farming, and reasonable self-sufficiency" (p. 171).

4. Reverence—where we honor the whole of creation with a deep sense of the sacred and how this manifests in the Earth.

5. Diversity and Equality. Wallis argues that particularly in the United States, integration of black and white has taken precedence over the concern for social justice. We should accept diversity and value equality first before we superficially integrate.

6. Peacemaking. Although conflict is inevitable in human affairs, war is not. We need to explore, more fully, non-violent solutions to conflicts.

7. Justice. This is at the center of any soulful approach to political life so that we deal more directly with the issues of poverty, inequality and discrimination.

8. Contemplation. Wallis suggests that contemplation allows political action to be rooted in wisdom rather than reactivity. He also states that "contemplation may be the most difficult thing for activists, yet it may be the most important thing" (p. 196).

9. Courage and responsibility. To confront the status quo and injustice requires courage and the willingness to take the first steps toward action. This involves a deep sense of personal responsibility toward change.

10. Integrity is vital to bringing soul and love back into the world. It means that conscience comes before success. It is interesting that the four leaders I have cited as examples of bringing soul into the world—Aung San Suu Kyi, Havel, Mandela, and the Dalai Lama—either went to jail or into exile because of their beliefs. Perhaps this could be a test of political authenticity whether the leader has been imprisoned or exiled for his or her beliefs.

11. Imagination. Building a better world requires our ability to imagine new possibilities much like Martin Luther King's "I Have a Dream" speech.

12. Reconstruction. This means moving from protest to building a new, and better world to live in. Wallis contrasts this principle to the one of "deconstruction," which tends to dominate academic thinking.

13. Joy. This is the sign that soul and love are part of political life. Love manifested in the world brings joy. Wallis describes the inauguration of Nelson Mandela as the new president of South Africa as an example of joy in public life.

14. Hope. Despair and apathy characterize public life. Soul and love brought into political life bring hope and the energy that accompanies hope.

The love that brings us into the world, then, is not just sentiment and warm feeling, but "force as the essence of the world itself, its substance, being, activity and destiny" (Sardello, p. 126). Sardello suggests this form of love involves bringing our dreams into reality. These dreams come from deep within our own soul and encourage us to create beauty, help those that are suffering, oppose injustice and oppression and the destruction of the natural world. From this perspective, we see the Earth as a source and not just resource, which has become the predominant worldview.

When we bring love into the world, we see ourselves in relationship with the Earth so that when we take something from the Earth we feel the need to replenish it. Sardello suggests that we can sense this form of love in our bodies and also in all the objects that exist on the Earth. All things are seen as symbols or signs of the soul of world expressing itself.

This sense is expressed in the Gnostic Gospel of Eve where Sophia says:

It is I who am you; and it is you who are me.
And wherever you are, I am there.
And I am sown in all; and you collect me from wherever you wish.
And while you collect me, it is your own self that you collect.
(Layton, p. 205)

Sardello calls this love that brings us into the world, "creative love." He suggests that marriage should be a balance between the intimate love of two people and also the creative love for the world. Here then the two partners see their relationship in a broader context of what they can give to the world through creative love.

WORK

Matthew Fox (1994) has made a strong case for the place of soul in work. At the very beginning of his book *The Reinvention of Work,* he states: "Work comes from inside out; work is the expression of our soul, our inner being. . . . Work is an expression of the Spirit at work in the world through us" (p. 5). We are beginning to hear about soul and spirit in the workplace, but the predominant language still focuses on restructuring and reengineering. John Dalla Costa (1995), who is consultant to corporations, suggests re-engineering has led to what he calls "change fatigue." The signs of change fatigue can be found where people in the corporation read the mission statement or see a video promoting the mission yet still feel "lethargic, uninspired, or even ashen" (p. 10). Another sign is that the corporation still looks to the outside consultant for answers rather than relying on internal resources.

The cover of a March 1995, issue of *Newsweek* had the title "Exhausted." It reported that the Annals of Internal Medicine stated that 24 percent of people who were surveyed complained of fatigue that lasts longer than two weeks.

> Fatigue is now among the top five reasons people call the doctor: People are frayed by the inescapable pressure of technology, frazzled by the lack of time for themselves, their families, their PTAs and church groups. They feel caged by their jobs even as they put in more overtime. We are fast becoming a nation of the quick or the dead-tired. "People are stretched financially, stretched in terms of time and stretched emotionally," says Leah Potts Fisher, co-director of the center for Work and Family in Berkeley, Calif. "So it doesn't take much for them to snap. " (Hancock et al. 1995, p. 58)

Corporate downsizing is partially responsible for this fatigue as today companies ask the employee to do one-third more work than their predecessors for the same pay and with less time off. Overtime work is at an all time high.

In our age of consumerism and materialism, addiction to work has become a major problem. Diane Fassel writes (1990):

> Everywhere I go it seems people are killing themselves with work, busyness, rushing, caring and rescuing. Work addiction is a modern epidemic and it is sweeping our land. . . . I call it the cleanest of all the addictions, it is socially promoted because it is seemingly socially productive. (p. 2)

Fassel states that the characteristics of workaholism are multiple addictions, denial, self-esteem problems, external referencing, in-ability to relax, and obsessiveness. The ultimate result of all of this, according to Fassel, is a spiritual bankruptcy.

> Spiritual bankruptcy is the final symptom of workaholism; it usually heralds a dead end. It means you have nothing left. . . . Fortunately,

when the workaholic downward spiral is reversed, spirituality is one of the first things recovering people regain. (p. 46)

It is this spiritual bankruptcy that has made some people talk about the importance of bringing soul into the workplace as a way of rebuilding it. By working from our souls, work takes on meaning and purpose. We have a sense that our work is our destiny as we have a deep sense that we are doing what we are supposed to be doing. When we find soulful work, we experience a deep joy. One woman who had started a bakery cooperative in her neighborhood put it this way:

> Work is an essential part of being alive. Your work is your identity. It tells you who you are. It's gotten so abstract. People don't work for the sake of working. They're working for a car, a new house, or a vacation. It's not the work itself that's important to them. There's such joy doing work well. (Terkel 1985, p. 470)

It is possible to experience joy when working. Educator John Holt became interested in music late in life and began to study the cello in his mid-forties. Despite this late start, he became quite a competent musician and it became central to his enjoyment of life. He speaks of his joy when finally music became part of his work, when asked by Ivan Illich to teach with him in Mexico:

> I did not go to Mexico to find an excuse or reason to play the cello. But these ideas, that grew out of my work there, became the bridge on which music-making came back into my life. . . . I hoped to find ways to make it something that all who wanted might take part in for themselves. In short, my love for music now seemed more and more joined to my love of teaching and to my deepest political concerns. The gap I had felt between my work and my hobby had disappeared. (pp. 185–86)

The joy from soulful work is akin to Joseph Campbell's oft-quoted phrase: "finding your bliss." Moore suggests that when we have a deep sense of vocation that there is an erotic element. He says. "Soul and the erotic are always together. If our work doesn't have an erotic tone to it, then it probably lacks soul as well" (p. 273). Eros in the Greek sense, connected to work means that our job has deep sense of purpose and energy.

The power of shared work can bring healing to people and communities. One story of such healing was told to me by a former coworker.

I returned home and was surprised to see my husband and next door neighbor at work cutting down a tree on their front lawn. Not surprised by the activity, the tree had been diseased for several years, but surprised by the presence of the neighbor. The man was a sullen and hostile loner, often drunk, and once had even viciously attacked my husband over a minor dispute. When I found an opportunity to ask my husband what was going on, he told me that he had been moved to offer the wood to the neighbor and hoped that this simple gesture might heal the relationship. The sullen man had responded that he would "earn" the wood by helping to cut. He wanted no favors. For some time the work progressed in silence apart from the sound of chopping and sawing. Then as they were stacking wood the neighbor finally broke the silence. "Stacking wood" he said "that's what they called it." "Called what?" was the puzzled response. "Called stacking the corpses in the camp," the neighbor replied. "What camp?" still puzzled. After a long pause, "Buchenwald" came out in a hoarse whisper. And then a flurry of memories of cleaning gas chambers and carrying the corpses in that hellish place came flooding out. The memories piled up with the stacks of wood. The talkative man became silent and the silent one allowed the words to flow along with the sweat of their labour. The back and forth of conversation resembled the movement of the Swede saw which they were using together. In the end it seemed that the instinct had proved correct. The simple offer of some timber and the shared work of cutting down the tree had healed the peace between the neighbors and perhaps had achieved a deeper healing.

Soulful work, then, can take on a sacred quality where healing may occur. In our fragmented world, where we have divided the secular and the sacred, our work is rarely seen in this way. Again, the ancients saw the everyday as a gateway to the eternal. Perhaps this is what is needed so desperately today: to see our work as actually a way of enlarging soul. This can be done by bringing our full attention to what we do. When this happens, presence arises with our attention. And with presence comes soul.

Unfortunately, the pressures and demands of work leave little time for attention and presence; instead we are pulled in multiple directions. With teachers, there are so many students to deal with, as well as the demands of administrators and parents. However, the more that we bring focus, attention, and presence to our work the more it becomes soulful. I will have more to say about this in my chapter on the soulful teacher.

Both Moore and Fox suggest that ritual be brought to the workplace to enhance soul. Fox (1994) suggests that ritual can be a field where the soul is brought alive in the workplace. Rituals can also connect work to the healing of the planet. Fox believes that rituals should reflect the new emerging cosmology and thus they should be participative and contain a spontaneous element. Perhaps the most important factor in ritual is that it fosters community. Fox (1994) says: "Ritual is an indispensable element for authentic community because in it we come together to name and celebrate, to lament, grieve and let go and to create and recreate our common task: the Great Work of the universe" (p. 262). Fox believes that workplaces that discover ritual will increase their productivity by 15 percent. More importantly, ritual increases creative energy. Rituals that Fox suggest include a new respect for Sabbath, universal sabbatical leaves. Fox relying on the work of Heschel (1951) believes that providing opportunities for rest, renewal, and ritual every seven days and seven years would help heal the dualisms that exist in ourselves and in our workplaces. These dualisms include "masculine/feminine; yin/yang; day/night; north/south; east/west; human/divine" (p. 277). The principles of ritual set out by Fox (1988) include:

1. Reset all of worship in a cosmological context.
2. Bring the body back.
3. Bring play back.
4. Make room for the via negativa—darkness, silence, suffering.
5. Awaken and nurture the prophet.
6. Bring participation back. (pp. 212–15)

Fox gives many examples of ritual. For example one is the Council of All Beings developed by Joanna Macy and John Seed. This consists of two circles of people facing one another where each person wears the mask of an endangered species. Each person speaks of his or her concern about the future of the planet and the earth. Other examples of including soul in the workplace and schools in particular can be found in the chapter on the soulful school.

I have mentioned the importance of attention and presence as of a way of bringing soul into our work and there will be more on this theme in chapter 8. However, on this same theme I would like to cite Emerson (1990):

> To finish the moment, to find the journey's end in every step of the road, to live the greatest number of good hours is wisdom. . . . Five minutes of today are worth as much to me as five minutes in the next millennium. Let us be poised and wise and our own, today. (p. 233)

Love and work are essential to our well-being and our souls. We need to approach both with a attention, presence and sense of mystery. Instead we have tended focus on control, manipulation and power (e.g., intimate terrorism). The result is a deep sense of dissatisfaction and dislocation. Bringing soul back to our love and work can allow us to approach both of these essential elements in a manner that can bring wonder, joy, and deeper feeling into our lives. We move now the second part of the book which explores more specifically how we can nourish the souls of our children in educational settings.

Part II

Nurturing Soul

4

Curriculum for the Inner Life

A soulful curriculum recognizes and gives priority to the inner life. It seeks a balance and connection between our inner and outer lives. Traditionally, schools have ignored the child's inner life; in fact, our whole culture tends to ignore the inner life. The child's and adolescent's lives are filled with TV, videos, computer games, with little unstructured time.

Children's lives often lack the environment where the inner life can develop. The research of Jerome Singer (1976) connects the development of inner life and behavior. He found that the risks of an undeveloped imagination include "delinquency, violence, overeating, and the use of dangerous drugs" (p. 32). This tendency appears early—as children who are impulsive and excessively dependent lack a developed inner life. Children who can use their imagination tend to be more relaxed and independent in their behavior. This trend continues into adolescence. Another study by Singer (1976) revealed that, in a child guidance clinic, imaginative children were less likely to be violent. Like the other children in the clinic, they were emotionally troubled, but they exhibited their difficulties in less aggressive ways than their unimaginative peers. These studies indicate that those individuals with an underdeveloped inner life seem to be more vulnerable to external stimuli.

Daniel Goleman, in his book *Emotional Intelligence* (1995) cites research by Walter Mischel that investigated whether a four-year-old child can control his or her impulses. This was tested by a task that involved resisting the impulse to reach for a marshmallow immediately. Delaying gratification for about twenty minutes was rewarded by the having two marshmallows rather than one. Mischel found that the ability to delay gratification at this early age was a powerful predictor of how students later performed in school and on SAT tests. Those children who were able to delay gratification scored 210 points higher, on average, than the children who grabbed the marshmallow.

One of the key factors in the development of healthy emotions and an inner life is the ability to monitor one's feeling state. One of the key skills is the ability to be aware of the body's sensations and feeling states so that anger and impulse do not get out of control (Goleman, p. 238).

Healthy emotional development involves empathy. Children who are ignored or abused often become candidates for criminal behavior. Adults who commit violent and abusive behavior are incapable of empathy. In contrast, children who are in the company of adults who are attuned to the child's emotions are more likely to grow up to be healthy and successful citizens. In short, empathetic adults help make empathetic children.

The questions remains: how can we support the development of a healthy inner life for students? I believe that we need to consider the creation of a curriculum of the inner life. Such a curriculum would provide a counterbalance to the current curriculum that completely focuses on the outer life (e.g., subject-based curriculum). In this chapter, I would like to discuss some of the elements of such a curriculum. These elements include (1) meditation, (2) visualization, (3) working with dreams, and (4) journal writing. Of course, there is some risk in working with the inner life. In some communities there has been strong opposition to some of the approaches suggested here. At the end of the chapter I discuss ways to minimize the risks but teachers need to use their judgment about which methods are appropriate to their classroom, school, and community.

MEDITATION

I have written extensively on the use of meditation, by teachers, to help them become more centered in their lives and in the classroom (Miller 1993, 1994). However, the use of meditation by students is a much more difficult and controversial issue. Despite the difficulties, more and more people are beginning to make the case for meditation in the schools. Iris Murdoch (1992), the renowned English novelist and philosopher, wrote:

> The damage done to inner life, to aloneness and quietness, through the imposition of banal or pornographic or violent images by television, is a considerable wound. *Teach meditation in schools* [my italics].

Some understanding of, and taste for exercises in detachment and quietness, the sense of another level, and another place, a larger space, might thus be acquired for life. Simply sitting quietly and calmly can be doing something good; subduing unkind or frenzied thoughts certainly is. Morality as the ability or attempt to be good, rests upon deep areas of sensibility and creative imagination, upon removal from one state of mind to another, upon shift of attachments, upon love and respect for the contingent details of the world. (p. 337)

Ms. Murdoch, who is certainly not part of the New Age movement, makes a very strong case for exploring meditation in schools. I personally feel that we do not need to teach young children to meditate. In many ways they already meditate with their focus on the here and now.

As children, the play of the sun on rippling water brought us before God's throne. Did you ever see an infant gaze at a light bulb or the moon? Spiritual techniques are discovered naturally by infants and little children: holding their breath, staring unblinking, standing on their heads, imitating animals, turning in circles, sitting unmoving; and repeating phrases over and over until all else ceases to exist. (Ram Dass 1978, pp. 62–63)

Older children and adolescents I believe could benefit from exposure to meditation in schools. Gina Levete (1995), who is associated with the Interlink Trust in England, has been working extensively in the area of meditation in the schools. She cites statements by fourteen- and fifteen-year-old children that indicate the need for the development of the inner life.

"I do lots of things but inside I feel alone."

"I hate doing nothing."

"I go to lots of parties but sometimes I think 'What's it all about?'"

"I always have the radio on for background noise."

"Walking is boring unless there is something at the end of it."

(p. 1)

Levete cites some studies that indicate the positive benefits of meditation for students. In one study, at a boys' school in the Middle East, secondary school students were split into two groups. The experimental groups meditated for the entire year on a daily basis and it was found that they performed better academically than the control group which did not meditate (Levete 1995, p. 2). Other research on meditation suggests meditation is helpful in relieving stress and lowering blood pressure (Benson 1976). Since many adolescents feel a great deal of stress related to schoolwork and or peer pressure, meditation could serve as a preventative to stress-related physical, emotional, or mental illness.

Levete argues that meditation could be used in schools if it is presented within a nonreligious framework. She cites the work of Jon Kabat-Zinn and Clive Erriker as people who have suggested that meditation can be practiced without reference to a specific religious tradition. Kabat-Zinn's techniques are connected to Buddhism but in his work with people who have chronic pain, he has found the meditation techniques can be adapted to be used without specific reference to religious or spiritual traditions. Kabat-Zinn's work has become well known through his books (1990) and his appearance on the Bill Moyers program *Healing and the Mind*. During his eight week program, individuals learn to practice basic breath meditation and mindfulness in a nondogmatic atmosphere. I believe that the same principles can be applied within an educational institution.

Levete suggests that meditation can be used in the elementary school with young children. To support her case she quotes the following individuals:

> *"Younger children naturally accept meditation because they don't come with so much baggage. By sixteen they tend to analyze and question the practice."*
> —Paul Moss, St. James Independent School

> *"I am constantly surprised at the capacity of young boys to sit still. Meditation is, I am sure, of enormous educational as well as spiritual benefit."*
> —David Lindsay, School chaplain, Haberdashers Askes
> (p. 12)

In this latter school, meditation was introduced as a result of the visit of a Franciscan friar in 1986. Ever since, the school has offered a fifteen-minute lunchtime meditation for those who want to participate. Numbers at this voluntary session range from six to thirty-six students. Meditation is also introduced to students in a class on Buddhism.

Levete also cites a teacher at a London primary school who stated that when meditation was introduced to seven- to eight-year-old students, she found that "by the fourth week children were noticeably quieter and more able to concentrate on meditating" (p. 12). Levete visited several schools in England where meditation was being used and came to the following conclusion. "After visiting a number of state and independent schools the overall impression is, that, provided students are presented with clear guidance, meditation for them is almost instinctive" (p. 13).

In general Levete found the following methods being used:

Following the Breath

Following the breath helps to calm and focus the mind quickly and stabilizes the body. The object of attention is the breath. Meditators are shown how to focus gently on the natural rhythm of the breath, the inhalation and the exhalation. The point of attention is usually either the tip of the nostrils or just below the navel. After breathing in and out deeply for a few times, the meditator sits quietly and focuses on the breath as it enters and leaves the body in its own rhythm. Although in theory this sounds an easy thing to do, in practice it can be difficult to sustain the focus for more than a few breaths. Once this simple technique has been learned, it can be applied at any time, particularly at times of stress.

Connecting to the Body

The object of attention is the body. The meditator learns to come down from the "thinking head" to sit as the "total body." The instructor guides the meditator to connect with the different parts of the body and then to extend awareness to the whole body and its ceaseless work being carried out without any conscious instruction. The meditator as the total body sits peacefully aware of the body breathing, renewing and moment.

Walking Meditation

In this practice, the object of attention is the action of slow walking. Total attention is placed in the action of the feet as they move and connect with the ground, harmonizing the action of walking step by step with the breath.

Meditating on a Sound or Word—Mantra Meditation

Here, the object of attention is a sound. Under the initial guidance of a teacher the mantra composed of sound, sounds, or word (s), is silently repeated over and over again until the mind settles into a natural quietness beyond the usual realm of mental activity, to a deeper level of inner being.

Meditation and Visualization

Under the guidance of a teacher this method of meditation uses visualization as a way to become more aware of the meditator's own potential and positive qualities. For example, the meditator may visualize the body filled with light, the warmth of the sun; or a positive quality such as kindness, patience, or goodwill held in the mind or directed outwards to other people. Visualization of this nature can be remarkably effective in inspiring a person to realize their own goodness. It can be particularly encouraging for deprived children to be aware of what they can offer to other people.

Meditation Observing the Mind

Although this is perhaps the most effective method of developing a sense of equanimity, it is a more advanced technique which requires a longer period of instruction and would only be suitable for older students. Here the object of attention is the mind's stream of thought. The meditator sits peacefully observing the flow of thought passing through the mind without the intervention of judgment, attachment or suppression. Instead the meditator simply notes each passing thought, and its impermanence when there is no conscious interference or attachment to it. (pp. 6–7)

Some of these techniques are discussed in more detail in chapter 8. The technique may vary but the object is to approach meditation with a mind that is both *relaxed and alert*. There is balance here for if we become too relaxed we can fall asleep; on the other hand if we try too hard to focus we can become tense.

Getting Started

Meditation in the school is probably best integrated with other activities. For example, meditation can be done as a centering activity before a stressful activity like taking a test. Similarly, it also can be utilized in conjunction with activities such as physical education or drama. Whether it is going to bat in baseball or performing one's dramatic role, centering allows the student to collect oneself.

One activity that can also be used to help students relax is progressive muscle relaxation. Here, the student is guided to relax muscles throughout the body, starting with the feet. The exercise involves first tensing, holding the tension, and then relaxing the muscles.

The teacher instructs the student approximately as follows:

Begin by sitting upright in a chair or lying on the floor. First, tense the muscles in the feet. Hold for a few seconds and then relax.

Exhale as you relax. Repeat this same process with the ankles, calves, thighs, buttocks, abdomen, chest, arms and hands, back, shoulders, neck, and facial muscles. After doing each part, then tense, hold, and relax the muscles in the entire body. Do this a couple of times.

Deborah Rozman (1976) describes different meditations that can be done with children. Below are a couple of these.

> Another concentration exercise consists of concentrating on the second hand of a watch or clock as it circles around. Every time a thought enters, let it flow by, don't let it carry you away from your point of concentration. Each thought is like a fishhook trying to catch you, the fish. See how long you can concentrate without getting hooked into thinking about something else. (p. 102)
>
> This second concentration exercise is one that can be very useful in stilling the mind any time of day and also can be practiced as you sit to meditate. Here, the meditator is asked to repeat a sound mentally over and over and again, and rhythmically tune it to the breath. We begin practicing it by sitting up in meditation posture as relaxed as we can be. Inhale through the nostrils slowly to a mental count of five to ten. Hold to the same count, and then exhale slowly to this same mental count. Be sure to do each part of the same count. Repeat five or ten times. When you are finished, relax and let the breath go. You will feel an inner balance and your breathing will be slowed down. This exercise is very good for hyperactive children and for people with nervous tensions. Now watch your breath as it naturally flows. Watch it as if you were watching someone else breathing. If it wants to stay in awhile, or out a while, let it. Don't control it or force it. Just let the breath do its own thing. When you feel like you are really hearing someone else breathing inside you mentally say the word Sa as the breath comes in and then Ha when the breath is ready to go out. . . . Sa again as it returns in and Ha again as it goes out. Really relax and yet focus at the same time. Repeat for several minutes building up the length of time you can do it as you practice. (pp. 103–4)

Rozman's suggestions are for elementary school children. If one is going to teach meditation to students at any level, of course it is important that the teacher be meditating.

VISUALIZATION/GUIDED IMAGERY

Visualization uses imagery as its principal focus. It has been used much more widely in the classroom than meditation, although not without controversy. I believe, however, that visualization is one of the ways that students can cultivate their imagination as it encourages the evocation of internal images. Research by Gaylean (1983) indicates that guided imagery can help students:

1. Be more attentive and less distracted.
2. Be more involved in the work being done in class.
3. Learn more of the material being taught.
4. Enjoy their learning experience more than before imagery was introduced to them.
5. Do more original and/or creative work, especially in art and writing.
6. Get along better with classmates.
7. Be more kind and helpful to one another.
8. Feel more confident.
9. Be more relaxed.
10. Do better on tests. (p. 25)

Different ways for using guided imagery in the classroom are described below.

Relaxation

Visualization can be used to help students relax and calm down. For example, I have heard teachers comment how they use it after recess when children are often excited. The teacher asks students to imagine a quiet, safe place where they like to be. Instead of yelling at students to quiet down the teacher can simply ask the students to go to their "safe place" in their imagination. A safe place is an image, or set of images, that bring peace and relaxation to the student. For example, some students visualize their room at home while others might visualize a favorite place in nature.

Guided imagery can also be used to relax students before a test. As mentioned above there is some research that suggests this improves student performance.

Storytelling

Have students close their eyes when you tell or read them a story. Let them develop their own inner imaginative response to the story. As I have already suggested, children's minds today are flooded with images from TV, videos, and computers. There is little opportunity for them to develop their own internal images. I grew up just before television took over. When I was young, people listened to radio and I can remember going up to my room at night turning off the lights. I listened to the radio in the dark and imagined how the story was unfolding. It felt magical. In Waldorf schools, the teacher sometimes lights a candle before he or she tells a story. This adds a feeling of ritual and magic to the storytelling process.

In a similar vein, a drama teacher told me that he has his students listen to the skit or drama on tape first so that they develop an inner imaginative response first before they attempt to act out the play. He said this adds immensely to the quality of the skit or drama.

Creative Writing

One of the most popular ways of using visualization is to take the students on a journey of some kind and then have them write a story about their journey. Below is visualization taken from *Spinning Inward* (1982) by Maureen Murdock that could be used in this way:

> *An Undersea Adventure*
>
> Close your eyes and focus your attention on your breath. (pause) Now imagine that you are walking down to the beach. It is a beautiful, sunny day and you enjoy the sound of the surf. (pause) As you walk along the beach you notice a trap door in the sand. You lift up the trap door and there is a stone stairway leading down under the sand. You walk down the stairway feeling perfectly safe, and find yourself in a long tunnelway. You walk through the tunnelway until you come to a room at the end of the tunnel. You enter the room which looks like a glass bubble. You realize that you are in a glass room under the sea. Beautiful colored fish are swimming outside. You notice that there is a submarine and a diving suit in the room for your use if you choose to venture out into the sea. There is also a pillowed chair in the middle of the room if you wish to sit down. You now have a minute of clocktime equal to all the time you need to enjoy all the wonders of the sea. (after a minute) Now it is time to return. (pause) You walk back through the tunnelway, up the stairs toward the sunlight. You close the trap door knowing that you can return here whenever you wish. You leave the beach and become aware of sitting here, fully present. I am going to count to 10. Join me at the count of 6, opening your eyes at 10, feeling fully alert and with full recollection of your adventure. 1 . . . 2 . . . 3 . . . etc. . . . . . . 10 (p. 60)

The student can also draw as well as write after the story. It is always important to "debrief" the students after the imagery exercise. This can be a period of silence, talking to other students about the experience, or writing about the experience in their journals.

Connecting Subject Matter with
Student's Inner Life

Guided imagery also allows the student to connect abstract subject matter with his or her own inner experience. For example my daughter was studying the water cycle in eight grade and after she studied it in her text, I read the following visualization to her.

> *A Guided Fantasy: Water Cycle*
> You will be peaceful and calm throughout this fantasy. You will have a pleasant, interesting and comfortable journey. No harm will come to you at any point. You will be perfectly safe at all times. You will always be able to do whatever you want to do. When your experience is over you will feel refreshed and relaxed, peaceful and full of energy.
>
> Allow yourself to flow with this fantasy. . . . Let go. . . . Give yourself permission to enter into it as completely as you can. . . . Take your own pace. . . . Go at your own rate.
>
> Visualize now, a large, calm lake at the base of some very high mountains. . . . The sun is rising slowly through scattered, pink clouds. . . . Enter into the peace and tranquillity of this scene. . . . Experience it as fully as you can. . . . Look all around you. See everything there is to see. . . . Listen to the early morning sounds. . . . Smell the fresh mountain air.
>
> Visualize the water.. . . . Now, you will BECOME the water. . . . You will become crystal clear, pure, transparent water . . . You are floating. . . . floating on the surface of the lake. Enjoy being there. Feel the water supporting you and buoying you up.
>
> The rising sun's glowing light penetrates the depth of your being. You are flooded with light. Let the light in. . . . Experience the light coursing through you. . . . Feel the sun filling your entire being with brilliant, bright light.
>
> As the sun rises higher, you begin to feel warmer and warmer. . . . You grow lighter and more energized. . . . You are expanding. . . . You begin to rise gently, invisibly. . . . You move higher and higher, until your are absorbed into billowy, white-gray cloud formations.
>
> Feel yourself carried along and rolled about by friendly, pillowy clouds. . . . Feel yourself rising with the clouds and swiftly moving upward towards the craggy mountain peaks.
>
> As you rise higher, a brisk, cold current of air transforms you—in an instant—into a shower of infinitely varied, brilliantly beautiful

snowflakes. . . . You move gently and ever so lightly downward towards the deep, soft snowbanks below. . . . As you gradually descend, the bright rays of the sun pass through you, and you begin glistening and flashing with the full color spectrum of the rainbow. Experience yourself in all your beauty and radiance.

You continue descending, lightly, airily and gracefully moving downward. . . . Gently, gently you are cushioned by the soft snowbank and your descent is ended. . . . Rest there in the sun and prepare for the completion of your journey. . . . Feel the heat of the sun. Let it in. . . . Warm yourself thoroughly. . . . Feel the warm energy flowing through you.

Fill yourself with sunlight. Allow it to flow through your entire being. . . . Feel the energy and power of this light. . . . Experience its radiance. . . . You have become a center of light.

You are rested now and refreshed. You are ready to move on. . . . You discover that the warm rays of the noonday sun have transformed you into crystal clear liquid. . . . You are fluid again . . . You begin moving downhill . . . now fast, now slowly . . . seeking your own way. . . . Feel your power as you flow.

You join other waters and move now right, now left . . . now over, and under . . . always following the path of least resistance . . . Flow at your own pace and find your own way back down to the lake.

You are nearing the bottom now . . . when you reach the lake, flow out onto the surface of the water and spread yourself out. Stretch, expand and float there. Feel the water supporting you. . . . Enjoy the exhilaration of having completed a varied and exciting journey. . . . Be aware of the wide range of your capabilities. . . . Be aware of your beauty and your power.

When you are ready, come back to yourself and to this room. Keep your eyes closed. . . . Spend some silent moments with yourself. You will feel refreshed and relaxed, energized and peaceful.

Continue to be yourself now . . . the person you are . . . and also remember that you are water. Remember your capabilities . . . your mobility . . . your power . . . your various modes of being. . . . Remember you are filled with energy and light . . . Allow yourself more often to experience yourself as fully as you have today. . . . When you are ready, open your eyes and make some contact with this room and with the people about you.

(Jack Sequist, cited in, *The Holistic Teacher,* pp. 103–105)

Here the student becomes the water, the clouds, snow, and water again, and thus abstract subject matter has become part of the student's inner life. Visualization allows learning to become holistic. Whitman said in his famous poem "The child went forth every day and that first object he looks upon, that object he became." Visualization allows the student to become the object he or she studies. This is not only central to learning at a young age, but it is part of the process that the artist and scientist goes through in their work. Consider Emerson's (1990) words: "A painter told me that nobody could draw a tree without in some sort becoming a tree" (p. 134).

The student can also visualize himself or herself in a variety of contexts including a historical one where the student imagines himself/herself as a historical figure. In English, students can imagine themselves as a character in a novel and in math, they can see themselves as a number being transformed. In *Mindsight* (1983) Beverly-Collene Gaylean describes several such visualizations. For example, if one has just studied Japan, the following exercise could be done:

> Close your eyes and imagine that you are traveling through space and time to Japan. . . . When you arrive there you notice all of the vibrant colors. . . . You notice everything about the environment . . . the houses . . . the types of transportation . . . what people do (pause). . . . You meet a friend who takes you home and prepares a meal for you. . . . You enjoy the smells and the tastes of Japanese food (pause). . . . Your friend introduces you to his/her family and friends and shows you what sports he or she plays. . . . You listen very carefully to the language spoken in Japan and to the songs the people sing (pause). . . . You spend a day with your friend at school noticing everything about school life in Japan (pause). . . . You then find yourself traveling back through space and time and arriving here in the classroom. . . . When I count to three . . . slowly open your eyes . . . remembering all the details . . . colors. . . . tastes. . . . sounds . . . and smells of life in Japan. . . . One . . . two . . . three . . . Write down what you remember from this experience. (p. 141)

After any guided imagery experience there should be time to process the activity. This can be done through writing about the experience, talking about the experience with another student or small group of students, or simply a short period of silence that allows for a transition to other classroom activities

Achieving Goals

Guided imagery can be used to help students achieve goals they have set for themselves. For example, they can see themselves doing well on a test or a job interview. It is helpful if students can be specific in what they visualize. They can visualize what clothes they are wearing and also how they are feeling. Below is visualization that might help students be more successful achieving a goal.

> Close your eyes and think of one thing you want to do well or better . . . (pause). . . . Now see yourself doing this thing with great success (pause). . . . Notice what your body looks like while you are doing this thing successfully. . . . Notice your attitudes about yourself and your abilities. . . . Be aware of your inner feelings . . . sensations as you do this thing successfully . . . (pause). . . . Feel yourself performing this action. . . . feel it in your whole being . . . (pause). . . . Notice how others appreciate this talent you have. . . . You have one minute of clocktime equal to all the time you need to image yourself performing this action successfully (pause). . . . Keep this image firmly in your mind and let it serve as a blueprint for your mind and body to follow (pause). . . . Always create this mental picture of yourself doing this thing successfully before you actually do it. . . . On the count of three . . . take a deep breath . . . exhale . . . and slowly open your eyes . . . alert and ready to work with this imagery. (Gaylean 1995, p.276)

Skill Development

This has been one of the most popular uses of visualization, particularly in the sports field. For example, the golfer can visualize a good golf swing or the baseball player a smooth swing of the bat and hitting the ball solidly. This same technique can be applied to music as the person sees himself or herself rehearsing the instrument in his or her mind.

Other skills that students can work on are spelling skills, writing skills, or doing a science experiment. Below is an example of how guided imagery can be used to help in spelling. This exercise focuses on the word astronaut but could be used with any word.

> Look at the board (or overhead, poster, other visual, etc.) and see the word ASTRONAUT. Repeat after me A-S-T-R-O-N-A-U-T. (People repeat letter by letter.) Now repeat the entire word ASTRONAUT. (People repeat the entire word.) This time close your eyes and listen to me spell the word. As I do, imagine you are writing each letter on your mind. If you wish, create a screen in front of your closed eyes, behind your forehead, and write the letters there. Take a slow, deep breath . . . hold your breath . . . and exhale any tiredness, distrac-

tion, or tension you may be feeling (pause). . . . Do this again. . . .
Take a slow deep breath . . . hold your breath. . . . and exhale any
tiredness, distraction or tension you may be feeling (pause . . . Re-
peat as needed). Now spell the word ASTRONAUT on your screen
. . . A . . . S . . . T . . . R . . . O . . . N . . . A . . . U . . . T. . . . Open your
eyes and check to see if you spelled it correctly (pause). . . . Now
close your eyes and let's do this again . . . Only this time let's spell
ASTRONAUT in colors . . . A . . . S . . . T . . . R . . . O . . . N . . . A . . .
U . . . T. . . . Open your eyes and check to see whether you spelled
ASTRONAUT correctly (pause) . . . . Take your pencil (or crayons,
paints, markers) and spell the word ASTRONAUT on your paper . . .
A . . . S . . . T . . . R . . . O . . . N . . . A . . . U . . . T. . . . Close your
eyes now and picture the whole word ASTRONAUT in front of
you. . . . Let's spell it out loud. . . . A . . . S . . . T . . . R . . . O . . . N
. . . A . . . U . . . T. . . . Whenever you spell any word you first need to
make a picture of it in your mind. That will help you to remember it.
Anytime you want to remember how to spell a word, you turn on this
film that you have made in your mind. (Gaylean 1995, p.101).

Interpersonal Skill

Students can also imagine themselves dealing well in the important
area of their interpersonal relationships. For example, if they see a
potentially troublesome meeting occurring with another person
they can visualize the meeting going well with a minimum amount
of conflict. Students can see themselves as relaxed and calm in
potentially troublesome encounters.

Attitude Change

Finally, guided imagery can be used to help students develop
healthy attitudes. Below is an exercise that focuses on happy
memories.

Close your eyes and take a deep breath . . . slowly breathe the air into
your lungs, and as you do this, notice how you become lighter and
lighter (pause). . . . As you breathe out, allow yourselves to feel a
sense of floating . . . floating away from this place where we are
now (pause). . . . Now take another deep breath . . . slowly filling
your lungs with a sense of lightness and brightness . . . Hold it . . .
Now exhale with a slight sigh and breathe out any tiredness. . . .
tension. . . . or distractions you might be feeling at this time
(pause). . . . Feel the peace within you . . . . the sense of well being

(pause). . . . Now picture the sun . . . warm and shining in a wonder-
fully clear sky . . . and image yourself breathing in the liquid warmth
from your sun. . . . With each breath you take you feel the sun filling
you with a wonderful light and making you feel lighter and lighter
. . . and brighter and brighter (pause). . . . Whenever you breathe
out, remember to breathe out any tiredness . . . tension or distraction you might be feeling at this time (pause). . . . At this time you
are going to use your mind to travel back in time to a moment when
you were very happy . . . a time when you were the happiest you can
ever remember being. . . . Everything was going well for you that day
or that moment . . . Go there now and relive this happy moment . . .
Experience this moment with all of your senses and feelings. . . . as if
this moment were happening right now. . . . If by chance nothing
comes to you at this time and you can't recall a happy moment. . . .
just remain calm within yourself and know that this moment may be
your happiest moment. . . . the moment that is best for you to remember. . . . Whatever you are experiencing at this time is fine. . . .
Notice what's going on in this happy memory. . . . Are you alone or
with others? . . . How are you feeling at this time? (pause) . . . Prepare yourself to return to us here in the room. . . . fully alert . . . and
refreshed . . . and ready to work with this imagery. . . . On the count
of three take a deep breath . . . hold it . . . and breathe out with a
slight sigh while gently opening your eyes. . . . Keep this happy memory fresh in your mind and let it refresh you anytime you wish. . . .
One . . . two . . . three. (Gaylean 1995, pp. 225–226)

All of the exercises described here can activate the inner life of the
student. Yet they should be done in a nonthreatening and inviting
manner. Students should not feel pressure to come up with a particular set of images or even to participate if they somehow feel uncomfortable with the exercise

Using Imagery in the Classroom

In preparing to do any visualization, it is helpful to begin with a
relaxation exercise. The student does a muscle relaxation exercise
(see pages 54–55) or some deep breathing. The teacher should
also make it clear to students that there is not a "right" set of images
but whatever comes into mind is appropriate and these images will
vary with each student. Students should be encouraged to close
their eyes during the experience since it is much more difficult to
visualize with the eyes open. A few students may not be comfortable
closing their eyes, however, and they should be allowed to keep

their eyes open. Students should also be told that they are in charge of their own experience. If they feel uncomfortable at any time they can open their eyes and stop the exercise for themselves.

In reading the guided imagery exercises allow approximately ten seconds where there are pause signs (. . .). Depending on the exercise it can sometimes help the process by playing soft music in the background.

After the exercise there should always be some debriefing or follow-up activity. For example, students can write about their experience in a journal or discuss their experience with other students in small groups of three or four students.

Guided imagery is most productive when it becomes part of the life of the classroom and is connected to the ongoing curriculum. It is least helpful when it is used as a "fill in" activity.

DREAMWORK

I have a dream that one day it will be universally acceptable for students of all ages to study their dreams. This work will be considered both valuable and meaningful in directing each student towards their greatest potential. Dream work will find a place in language arts, secondary English, art, drama, music and religious studies. I look forward to a day when dreams will be considered an important method of holistic education, one that nourishes the mental, physical and spiritual needs of each student. I envision a time when dream work and meditation in education will not be considered unique, mystical or mysterious. Teachers will not only feel comfortable engaging in this work, but experience with awe and satisfaction the wisdom it brings to their students' lives.

—Marina Quattrocchi (1994, p. 1)

Much of this section is based on the work of Marina Quattrocchi, a secondary school teacher, whose doctoral thesis focused on students' dreamwork. Generally, dreams have been excluded from the school curriculum because they are considered trivial or too private to bring to the classroom. Wood (cited in Quattrocchi, 1999, p. 6) identifies some of the barriers to the exploration of dreams in education. First, he believes that dreams are not seen as meaningful. If they are considered meaningful, this meaning is limited to artistic creation. Another reason for not using them in the classroom is that teachers do not see themselves as qualified to deal with dreams. A final concern is that dream work may release uncontrollable forces of the unconscious. However, there is support for the use of dreams in educational settings (Bastian 1987; Christie 1983; Doll 1982; Grumet 1988; Haye 1975; Jung 1974; Kincher 1988; and Ullman and Zimmerman 1979). Ullman and Zimmerman argue:

> It is not dangerous to work with dreams but, it may be dangerous not to. The issue of danger is not inherent in the nature of dream work unless the work is pursued without respect for the authority of the dreamer. When we have a dream we are ready to deal with it. The danger, as far as I'm concerned, is not of any threat unleashed by the dream but of failing to see what the dream sets before us. (p. 317)

In conducting her research on dreams Quattrocchi (1994) identifies her implicit theories. These include:

1. We have disregarded dreams in our society and delegated them as irrelevant and nonsense.
2. Dreams have played a significant role in many previous civilizations, e.g., biblical times, Indians, ancient Egyptians, Greeks and Senoi dream interpreters were highly respected individuals in these civilizations.
3. Dreams ceased to be valuable guides for self-direction approximately 400 years ago when dreams were grouped together with the occult, witchcraft, Satanism, telepathy and astrology.
4. Working with dreams is like learning a foreign language. At first you may remember only words or phrases. It does not make sense in the beginning and requires dedication and perseverance. Gradually the words fit together into a meaningful language.
5. Greater insight into our dreams can develop through discussion with family and friends. Because we are personally involved with the content, it is difficult for us to be objective.
6. We do not need an expert/psychologist to analyze our dreams in all cases. Although experts can provide deeper insights there is a sagacity within our unconscious that emerges with dream work.
7. At the heart of our dreams there is an inner wisdom that we can access if we pay attention to our dreams.
8. The language of dreams is highly symbolic. These symbols MAY come from our personal consciousness or from the collective unconscious. Working with these symbols provides greater insights and meanings.

9. Dreams are a powerful tool for greater self-direction and self-awareness.
10. An understanding and personal exploration of dream symbols MAY lead to a greater understanding of symbolism in art, religion, mythology, poetry, literature, and theater.
11. Creativity may be enhanced through dreams and dream images. This creativity may be expressed through art, dance, music, drama, poetry, and narrative writing. (pp. 3–4)

These assumptions provided the basis for Marina's work in the classroom. If one is going to work with dreams it is important to examine the underlying assumptions in doing dream work.

According to Jung, dreams can allow us to access the Self. Images that come forth in dreams can indicate messages from the Self. Sanford (1968), a Jungian analyst and Episcopal priest, explores this concept:

> There lives within us what seems like an unconscious source of wisdom which helps us to see ourselves in a different perspective from what we had before and which seems to work toward the healing and wholeness of the personality. This wisdom uses dreams as communications, and it enables us to understand consciously these symbolic messages. (p. 38)

Dee (1984) has comments that are also relevant here:

> A genius is a visionary and a visionary is a dreamer. We are all dreamers and we may all be visionaries but we are not all geniuses. The difference between the da Vincis of this world and others is that they can pluck a thought or an idea that comes to them in the still of night, in a dream and create from it reality. To them the true world is their inner world. Above all, they are good listeners, not only to other people but [to] that small, quiet voice within. (p. 39)

Dreamwork is based on the assumption that within each person there is a "source of wisdom" that allows that person to work with dreams and internal images.

Working with dreams in the classroom is based on the assumption that the teacher does not have to be an expert in dream theory. For example, Ullman and Zimmerman (1979) argue that "many nonprofessionals work very effectively in a more intuitive way" (p. 245). With regard to education, Clark (1975) states "the teacher need not be an expert in dream interpretation, but he must know how to listen and maintain a nonjudgmental attitude. He must also be willing to acknowledge his own ignorance" (p. 502). Ullman and Zimmerman (1979) add: "For parents and teachers who agonize over the distance between themselves and their children, dreams offer a warm and honest connection" (p. 319). Doll (1982) worked with dreams of teachers going to night school. She had them examine their dreams and analyze any patterns that they saw. She suggests that dreams could provide a way of exploring important images in the students' lives.

> A curriculum that uses dream speech provides new dispensation for learning about the self and culture. A course could be designed from the inside out, turning current curriculum practice around. Teachers skilled in following images could connect students first to their prime dream images and then to cultural expressions of these same prime images. In such a way a student is brought together with those symbolic expressions that have the most deep, personal meaning. Nor should these images be drawn from one period or genre. Once they have been elicited from dreams they could be researched in various fields and media. Students could present their research in a variety of ways: expositionally, fictionally, artistically, dramatically. (p. 201)

Christie (1983) conducted research on dreams with two groups of ninth-grade students. One group did creative writing starting with beginning sentences, while the other group did creative writing based on dreams. Christie found that the stories written from dreams demonstrated greater self-revelation. Students also indicated that dreams could also help in other creative areas such as poetry and dance.

Quattrocchi in her review of the literature on dreams suggests that the focus on dream work in the classroom should not be on interpretation of dreams but simply appreciation. Students need to learn to simply pay attention to their dreams. As they examine the images from the dreams, meanings may arise, but meaning should not be deliberately sought. It should simply be discovered in a more spontaneous way. Ullman and Zimmerman (1979) describe this process: "Your dream images are part of an intrinsic self-healing that is available to you. Their meanings become clear not through gimmickry but through steady honest work. And the reward of finding the meaning embedded in the images is often joy and hope" (p. 18)

Some practitioners suggest that the following questions can be used in dealing with dreams. Crisp (1990), for example, provides the following questions:

1. What is the background to the dream?
2. What is the main action in the dream?
3. What is your role in the dream?
4. Are you active or passive in the dream?
5. What do you feel in the dream?
6. Is there a because factor in the dream? (For example, you do not go through a door because you are afraid in the dark.)
7. Am I meeting the things I fear in my dream?
8. What does the dream mean?
9. What can I learned if I amplify or act out the dream?
10. Can I alter the dream to find greater satisfaction? (Cited in Quattrocchi 1994, p. 64)

Kincher suggests seven questions:

1. Do certain words or images dominate my dream?
2. Is anything wrong in my dream?
3. Have I had this dream before?
4. Did anything important happen on the day before the dream?
5. How did I feel on the day before the dream?
6. What did I eat before I went to bed?
7. What do I think my dream is telling me?

(Cited in Quattrocchi 1994, p. 65)

Marina Quattrocchi's study focused on her work with thirty high school students. She distributed a booklet on dreaming to the students. Information for this booklet was taken from *Dreams Can Help: A Journal Guide to Understanding Your Dreams and Making Them Work for You* by J. Kincher. The booklet dealt with dream theory, keeping dream journals, and guidelines for understanding dream symbols. Quattrocchi began each class by discussing material in the dream booklet. Her overall process for working with dreams included having students:

1. Writing down or recording your dream
2. Reflection thinking about your dream
3. Discussing or retelling a dream: probing
   sharing
   questioning

4. Deeper reflection. Reveling in a dream through poetry
               drama
               art
               music
               symbolic
               research
               active
               imagination
5. Revelation: Discovery of meaning "ah ha" . . . click of awareness
6. Acting upon a dream message resolution
         action
         ritual
7. Process repeats or begins again.

              (Quattrocchi 1995, p.273)

Students begin with keeping their own journals. Quattrocchi (1995) puts five questions on the board to help the students in writing their journals

1. What is the overall feeling or emotion you are left with? (This can be similar to the overall tone or mood of a novel.)
2. Note any symbols that appear.
3. Give your dream a title (this can be done days or weeks later).
4. Write down everything you remember, regardless of how insignificant or trivial you feel it is.
5. Pay attention to strong or significant colors in your dreams.

The beginning of each class would be devoted to discussing a page of the dream booklets and the discussion of students' individual dreams. At first students were reluctant to share dreams but after a while they became more comfortable sharing their dreams. Quattroacchi (1995) describes this process.

> After a student told their dream, classmates could volunteer their thoughts regarding the dream. Our goal was to generate many possible meanings. Attempts were not made to analyze the dreams. This was always left to the student. Often I would share my own dream, particularly if a theme or situation was similar to one a student had just shared. Students loved this part of the class. As the weeks passed, I was continually amazed at their openness, honesty and insights. (p. 120)

At the end, the students developed a paper, or a presentation, based on an examination of three of the dreams that they had.

Many of the students used the arts to present their dreams; for example students used songs and poetry to present their dreams. In this way the dreams stimulated creativity in the students. In reviewing the papers and presentations Quattrocchi (1995) found the following outcomes:

1. Increased awareness and insight into their present problems, struggles and emotions.
2. Problem solving abilities increased particularly with relationships. For example, one student had a dream that showed the chaos that resulted from her decision to "sneak around" with a boyfriend that her parents did not approve of. Images in her dream convinced her to end the relationship.
3. Better class rapport. Quattrocchi found that as the dreams were discussed in class that rapport improved in three areas: "student-student, student-teacher and student class."
4. Evidence of personal growth through confronting the shadow. The most frequently recurring dream was being chased by a sinister figure. Students were able to work with their dreams to confront the shadow figure and thus grow.
5. Increased creativity. Some students took the opportunity to be creative in relation to their dreams. Two students brought in music that they felt helped represent the dreams they had. Other activities included writing poetry, drawing pictures and dramatizing the dream through a skit.
6. Spiritual links were made by many students. For example, one student dreamed that time was sliding by and that she needed to wake up to her spiritual needs.
7. Prophetic dreams. Students had dreams that they felt predicted the future in some way. (p. 147)

One student summarized the results of working with dreams:

> *My feelings regarding the significance of dreams has changed drastically over the course of this assignment. Dreams are an important part of our life, if we could better understand our dreams we could better understand ourselves. Dreams usually reflect the problems we cannot deal with in our conscious mind and sometimes even give us a solution to the problem. To believe dreaming is not important is unintelligent considering the effects on individuals deprived of their dreams, their physical and mental health fails.*
>
> *The only difficulty I had with this assignment was to remember my dreams. Once I remembered my dreams, I did not find it extremely difficulty to interpret them. Interpreting or questioning what was dreamt is very important based on*

two main reasons. If we can see what problems upset us we can eliminate them when we are awake; this will make us feel better. The second reason why we should try dream interpretation is life interpretation. Dreams are an insight into our emotions and explanation of why we do the things we do. I definitely intend to continue keeping a dream diary which I believe will better my life and my understanding of my life. (p. 166)

Quattrocchi interviewed six students to supplement her findings. The interviews supported and extended her findings from the classroom work.

Like imagery and meditation the teacher must provide a "safe" environment for students and not attempt to manipulate the student in any way. Again safeguards for using dreams will be explored at the end of the chapter.

AUTOBIOGRAPHY/JOURNAL WRITING

Having students write about themselves is another activity that can enhance soul. One vehicle for doing this is having them write their personal histories. A good example of this process comes from the teaching of Jessica Siegel whose work is described in the book *Small Victories* (Freedman 1990). Jessica taught at Seward Park High in Manhattan which mostly serves the children of immigrants to the United States. In this school of 3,500 students, where the odds seem overwhelming, 92 percent of the graduates go on to higher education.

Jessica teaches English and one of the most important parts of her curriculum is having students write an essay on "Who Am I?" She wants them not to write the superficial essay on "What I Did on My Summer Vacation"; instead, she wants the students to share their thoughts and feelings. There are several benefits to this process. First, she has seen a powerful autobiographical essay help a student get into college or university. For example, one student Vinnie Mickles had a 69 percent average yet was able to get into the State University of New York at New Paltz. Vinnie had never met his biological father and his mother had been in and out of psychiatric hospitals a half-dozen times. He lived in an apartment with his mother where there was no heat and it was so cold that his hands froze and cracked so badly that they bled. The landlord was trying to force out the tenants so that he could raise the rent or sell the building. Because of these conditions, he could not concentrate on his work. Jessica recognized his potential and passed him. He entered the Marine Corps after graduating from Seward. After two years in the Corps he came back to Jessica and wanted her help to get into a university. Jessica had him write his autobiography and "he delivered a devastatingly dispassionate tale of his mad mother, his absent father, his icy apartment" (p. 48). On the basis of his autobiography Vinnie was accepted at the State University of New York.

Through the autobiography Jessica gains a much more complete view of the student. In short, she can begin to see the student as a whole person. Her instructions to the class:

> Think about your past experiences. Jot down ideas, memories, key words, whatever thoughts come to mind when I'm talking. Think of a personal object that's important to you. Why? Think about someone who has had a big effect on you. What happened? What did they say? List four or five words that describe your feelings. Pick one and illustrate with a memory from you past. List five things you're proud of. Choose one and say why it's important to you. Remember the first time you did something that stands out in your mind. Describe the incident. How did you feel about it? Have you changed in the last five years? Why? How? What made you the person you are today? (Freedman 1990, p. 51)

Her students write of so many events that have affected their lives. Divorces, beatings, adultery, the near death of a parent, and even becoming a parent. One student described how becoming a father and watching his child come out of his wife's womb was the most wonderful experience of his life.

Another story from a Chinese student moved her deeply. He tells his story of how he became a gang member and was involved in robberies and muggings. One of his friends tried to talk him into leaving his gang but he refused. One day he was walking with this friend and the two were attacked by another gang. When Lun Cheung woke up at the hospital, he learned that his friend had died in the attack. Lun Cheung gave up the gang life and is attempting to improve his life in many ways.

Finally, another student described a difficult life with her foster parents. They fought and then divorced. She lived with her foster mother for awhile but life was so difficult she moved to a group home on the recommendation of her social worker.

After reading these autobiographies Jessica experiences a strong sense of connection to her students:

Every year she finishes the autobiographies the same way. Her students are heroes. Her heroes, even some who fail the coursework. Could anyone else understand that? How they fill her with awe. How they, yes, inspire her. (Freedman 1990, p. 68)

Autobiography, then, can provide a silent bond between teacher and student. Clearly, such work must be handled with sensitivity and care by the teacher. An insensitive or careless remark could hurt a student and sever the student-teacher relationship.

Other teachers use the journal as a place where students can reveal their thoughts and feelings on a more regular basis than through the autobiography. Yet other journals are designed to be kept in a more academic way. These reflective journals usually contain the students' reflections on what they are reading and studying in class. It might include their reactions to a novel or a science experiment. In contrast, a soul journal would contain the students' feelings and thoughts as they go through each day. A soul journal focuses on the student's inner life. Of course, it is important to define who is going to read the journal. There may be portions or elements that are not open to anyone else.

FINAL THOUGHTS

All of the approaches suggested here should be introduced in a nonintrusive and invitational manner. There should be no sense of coercing students to reveal their inner life. A tone can be set where people do not feel compelled or forced in any way. Some students may prefer not to reveal anything and this is fine as each student finds his or her own trust level with different teachers. Here are some things to help keep the use of these techniques from being manipulative or intrusive.

1. Tell students that they can opt out of the experience. During meditation, visualization, or dreamwork the student can just sit quietly and read if they do not want to participate.
2. Emphasize that students are in control of their own experience. If they feel uncomfortable with an exercise at any time they can open their eyes and stop the experience.
3. Explain that there is no "right answer" in these exercises and that whatever arises for the individual student is appropriate for him or her.

4. As a teacher, be attentive and present to the students when they discuss their experience. This helps create a safe climate for students.

5. Allow time or provide an opportunity to "debrief" the experience after the exercise. Avoid moving directly from inner work to another activity without some "transition" time.

6. Always provide a rationale and context for the experience so that students understand why this is happening.

7. It is also helpful if the teacher reveals something of his or her personal life. Teachers can share stories that let students into their lives. Emerson (1990) wrote about a preacher but it can be applied equally well to teachers:

> He had lived in vain. He had not one word intimating that he had laughed or wept, was married or in love, had been commanded, or cheated, or chagrined. If he had ever lived and acted, we were none the wiser for it. The capital secret of his profession, namely, to convert life into truth, he had not learned. (p. 16)

I share my story (Miller 1994, pp. 154–60) in my classes and have found that it has had a positive impact on students. Many students have told me that they are glad I told them about certain important events in my life. Again the classroom is not a place for extensive self-disclosure but simply a place where we can, on occasion, drop the role of teacher and simply be a human being. The more we can succeed in this task the more satisfying our job becomes as we find we can more deeply connect to our students.

5

Arts Education and the Soul

The arts have always been among the ways that human beings have nurtured soul. Unfortunately, the arts in schools have been marginalized so that we can pursue the "basics." The arts don't seem to fit the agenda to produce citizens to compete in a global economy. This flies in the face of mounting evidence that suggests that the study of the arts actually increases the growth of neural pathways, aids in improving memory, and promotes creative problem solving.

As a 1994 report of the Royal Conservatory of Music (Toronto) states:

> Our culture's concept of "art for art's sake" is a recent development. In most cultures, including, until recently our own, the arts have been a medium to express who we are and what we know about ourselves. The arts were central and accessible, and easily woven into a child's learning experience. The thickly drawn line between arts and non-arts, so evident in our schools today, simply did not exist
>
> That we have relieved the arts of their central role in education is a tragedy. The arts represent a natural and experiential way for children to learn. (p. 20)

VISUAL ART IN WALDORF EDUCATION

I will begin this chapter with a discussion of art instruction in Waldorf schools because I know of no other approach that integrates art into the curriculum in such a complete manner. For the Waldorf teacher, art is not just a subject but integral to almost everything in the curriculum. For Rudolf Steiner, the founder of Waldorf education, art is essential to the unfolding of the inner person. Richards (1980) states that art involves:

> a certain way of seeing the child, a feeling for life, an intuition of the connections between the inner processes of forming and their outer

expression. . . . A sense of awe rises in the presence of the child, as in the presence of a poem one hears forming in one's inner ear. (p. 69)

For Steiner, creative expression was linked with the cosmos itself. In his autobiography he quoted a friend as saying:

People do not have as much as an inkling of the real significance of the creative power within the human soul. They do not realize that the creativeness of man is an expression of the same cosmic power that creates in nature. (Cited in Wilson 1985, p. 72)

In discussing Waldorf education, it is important to be aware of the stages of human development that Steiner defined as the stages that form the basis for the curriculum. Each stage involves an awakening. The first stage (ages 0–7) is the awakening and development of the physical aspect of the person. The child moves his or her limbs and so Waldorf education encourages children of this age-group to move and clap their hands when learning to count. When learning to draw, the child uses large block crayons so that the color can almost be felt as the child draws. In learning to draw forms and lines, the child's movement is also emphasized. Steiner believed that there were three main aspects of human existence: willing, feeling, and thinking. In getting the limbs to move, the will is exercised.

The next stage (ages 7 to 14) begins when the child's baby teeth give way to the adult teeth. In this stage, the focus of development is on feeling and imagination as development is centered in the heart and trunk area. It is important that the child hears stories, fables, and legends that contain rich and meaningful images that nurture the child's inner imaginative life. The teacher is also important to this development as Steiner felt that the student should have the same teacher through this period so a deep sense of trust can develop between teacher and child.

From ages 14 to 21, the focus shifts to thinking, as the adolescent explores questions of meaning and is often attracted by ideas that can engage his or her passion. Artistic activity at this stage is integrated around the increasing intellectual concerns of the person.

Stephen Sagarin (1992) teaches art at a Waldorf school and describes in detail how he approached the art classroom in grades 6 to 12. He states that art is not used to express "pent up" feelings but is seen as relating to "the development of children's capacity to observe and distinguish vital forces in nature and in themselves.

The active experience of a creative idea is more essential than the art 'product' itself. The development of the student herself is key" (p. 19).

In grade 6 Sagarin has the student work with watercolors on paper that has been soaked in water for a few minutes and sponged dry. He asks the students to follow what he is painting but he does not tell them what the subject is. Eventually, the students discover the subject; however, by keeping the subject secret, the student begins to "see" the art in a different way. Sagarin states: "Rather than seeing in the conventional, undeveloped sense of what they think they see, they learn to see things as they are. All of, what was merely a long, thin triangle may become a river" (p. 20). Even though the students follow the teacher's lead, each picture comes out differently. The students use different brushes and different amounts of water in the colors. All this combines to give a unique effect.

Sagarin also has the students combine colors to form new colors. For example, blue and yellow are combined to make green. After mixing the colors, Sagarin asks the students if they think the colors are now balanced. If they feel the color is too weak, they will add more blue to make the green stronger. Sagarin states: "By talking about the painting in terms of balance, the balance of light and dark, warm and cool, we approach a sense for color harmony and discord" (p. 20). According to Sagarin, some students prefer discordant paintings while others prefer more balance and harmony in the paintings. He begins the course with two colors but gradually adds others till there are six colors (three primary and three secondary). The rest of the colors the students must mix themselves.

The overall approach is based on the work of Goethe (1970), who argues that color arises from the interaction of light and dark. Goethe believes that the warm colors—red, orange, and yellow—arise when light passes through a darkening medium. The cool colors—blue and purple—arise when darkness is seen through a light-filled medium. Green appears when the two types of color overlap. When the colors mentioned are painted around a circle, they form a color wheel. Sagarin then describes how the color wheel is used in the classroom:

> As the course progresses we often "step out" of the color wheel for a day or two to include black (a volcano erupting at night) or brown (an aqueduct over a sluggish, muddy river in the heat of a Roman summer). As much as possible, we paint scenes that arise from the

students' main lesson study at the time of the course. . . . Often this is the study of ancient Rome, although it can be the geography of the north (Tundra, fir trees, icy mountains, ice floes) or other subject. The point of the course is to deepen the children's capacity to see the world as a formation or product of color. (p. 21)

The main lesson that Sagarin refers to is taught every morning for about two hours and can focus on a period of history or some story, legend, or myth.

In seventh grade the students study the Renaissance. According to Sagarin, students at this age have a fascination with this period of history as they are intrigued by the possibilities of exploring and mastering many areas of endeavor simultaneously (e.g., music, sports, art, academics, drama). Linear perspective is taught within this context. Sagarin comments: "The world is open to them the way it was to the thinkers and explorers of the Renaissance. The discoveries of linear perspective challenge seventh graders, but they persevere readily. It's so 'cool' to be able to draw buildings and roads that look 'real'" (p. 21).

The class begins with focusing on how the "vanishing point" in a picture appears to move with the observer. Sagarin draws a road vanishing into the distance and the students follow the teacher's lead. Again pictures differ as "some draw a dirt road with car tracks in it, while others draw a black asphalt strip with a double yellow line down the middle" (p. 21). Students also use light differently with some drawing the picture at midday while others focus on nighttime. Here the students use colored pencils for the work instead of water colors.

In the next grade, eighth grade, one art project involves having the student make a model or caricature of the human face with clay or papier-mâché. Sagarin believes this process is helpful, as students in these grades are in the process of going through adolescence and are just finding out who they are. Sagarin comments: "By imaginatively creating, or re-creating the character of others, students begin the process of sorting out their own personalities" (p. 21). Students in other subjects are studying the biographies of men and women in history and science, a process that allows them to reflect on the ways in which lives unfold.

In preparing the model, the students first study the human face and its proportions. This process can lead to some insight on the subjectivity of our perceptions as students discover, for example, that the eyes are central in the head and not near the top as is the usual perception. The face is drawn from both the front and side. Various face forms are examined, including the masculine and feminine face, as well as stereotypes such as the intellectual or "egghead" or the sensitive "artiste."

After these explorations, the students start working with the clay to form a face. Three to five pounds are used, a mass ample enough to allow the student to shape the face with his or her hands, which renders the experience more direct and immediate. They start by forming a sphere and then gradually work on the features. Sagarin asks them to describe the features from the start or, "otherwise, many students will putter around without a plan and choose only to exaggerate what has already been malformed by their efforts" (p. 22).

Sagarin finds that the first efforts of the student often reveal a face that is in many ways a self-portrait. For example, a student who sees herself as an intellectual will often make a high forehead while a student with low self-esteem will sculpt a face with an exaggerated, slack jaw.

Finally, Sagarin asks the student to express some emotion in the face such as "pain, sorrow, joy, boredom, curiosity" (p. 22). After the students have expressed one emotion, Sagarin then asks them to do the opposite emotion. He says: "It is certainly good for someone who is melancholic to immerse himself in modeling some melancholic expression (which he will usually choose to) and then to have to model the opposite—either great joy or fiery intensity" (p. 22).

By ninth grade, students tend to see things in terms of black and white just as they tend also to the extremes of either love or hate. The Waldorf school allows the student to explore this tendency in art through black and white. Sagarin has them make block prints, which are black and white, but also allows the opportunity to reconcile the polarities. Sagarin also encourages the student to select something from the natural world to work with, such as a human or an animal. These objects are also drawn in their natural surroundings.

Sagarin's students start with line drawings before doing the block prints. This way, they can explore more freely the relationship between black and white and light and dark. He also encourages them to look at the work of other artists such as Dürer and Picasso. Both artists worked at times in wood block prints but produced very different work. Picasso chose to distort the natural through his particular artistic vision while Dürer managed to produce almost photographic results, such as his famous woodcut of a hare in which it is said that "you can see every hair."

In working with the wood, the students cannot erase lines so they must think carefully about what they are doing. Sagarin states:

> The carving process, almost painful for some students during which one must be conscious of every move, every stroke, helps students become conscious of the effects of their labor. We strive for self-consciousness, not in the sense of stage-fright, for example, but for a healthy sense of self in relation to the world. (p. 23)

In the tenth grade, Sagarin teaches the students Roman calligraphy. He finds that calligraphy is humbling, yet also provides a sense of accomplishment. Sagarin starts by teaching students the appropriate posture and the way to hold the pen. He finds that some students take to the calligraphy easily, while others struggle to get an even flow of ink onto the page. Sagarin believes that "because of the subtle and precise gestures necessary to draw letters well, perceptual problems often manifest themselves here, and I believe the practice of calligraphy aids development of two-dimensional awareness in ways that the other arts cannot" (p. 23).

In the eleventh grade, the students study medieval romances. One of the art projects that Sagarin has selected as complementary to this study is the construction of stained glass windows. Using Goethe's theory of colors again, students experiment with color. They also study atmospheric color in the paintings of Turner, Monet, and others in order to obtain an understanding of general principles of atmospheric color. In working with glass, differently colored pieces are interspersed to achieve a blending and balancing of color. This underscores earlier work with the color wheel and previous exercises with perception. As colors are blended in the stained glass project, perception of overall atmospheric color change and the whole effect undergoes a metamorphosis. Students are nearing the end of puberty so it seems appropriate that one of the themes that is explored during this year is metamorphosis. They are encouraged to look back at who they were and who they might become. Sagarin comments: "By observing atmospheric color in the stained glass class, they experience a daily and seasonal metamorphosis from which they can learn" (p. 24).

In twelfth grade, students sculpt life-size busts in clay. This is similar to work done in grade eight but now the emphasis is on character rather than caricature. The students can choose from three types of projects: (1) sculpting a bust of a famous person, (2) copying another artist's sculpture, or (3) portraying a particular emotion in the sculpture. Sometimes this sculpture work is done in relation to architecture. This leads to a discussion of how architecture can be an outer expression of inner structures.

Art, then, in Waldorf education allows the student to witness and facilitate his or her own transformation. Clearly, art, here, is not just self-expression, but something that engages the whole student. The intellectual, emotional, and physical faculties are called upon and developed.

DRAMA/IMPROVISATION

Many of my students have argued that drama is one of the most holistic subjects since it can combine several subjects (e.g., English, history, art, and music) as well as engaging the whole person (e.g., the intellectual, emotional, physical, and spiritual). Neville (1989) makes a case for using Moreno's approach to drama, which is a form of psychodrama. Jacob Moreno grew up in Vienna when Freud expounded his theories of psychoanalysis. However, Moreno believed that Freud's approach was too narrow and reductionistic. Instead, he developed an approach to personal growth that was based on role-playing and improvisational theater. Neville believes that his approach can easily be transferred to schools.

> It is not uncommon now to find psycho-dramatic techniques in use in schools and preschools, by teachers who claim no competence as "therapists" but who nevertheless find psychodramatic techniques a valuable means of assisting the learning and emotional growth of their students. (p. 195)

Psychodrama involves acting out situations that are emotionally connected to students. The teacher directs or supervises that improvisation. Below is an example of such a situation. To begin we need:

The Director
The person who guides the psychodrama. The role demands a degree of confidence, authority, sensitivity and creativity, but neither mystical insight nor magical powers.

The Stage
The area that is set aside for the enactment. In "classical" psychodrama, this is a tiered platform with spotlighting and such effects. In the classroom it is usually just a cleared space. Those who find a

degree of ritual productive may have a square of carpet set aside for such occasions.

The Protagonist
The child who is the central actor in the psychodrama, and whose experiences (or conflicts, or problems) are to be acted out.

Director: Who's got a play for us today?
Billy: My dog went into Mrs. David's place and he wouldn't come out, so I went in to get him. And Mrs. David. . . .
Director: OK, Billy. This can be Mrs. David's place. How did you get in?
Billy: Through the gate.
Director: Well, then show us the gate. *(Billy indicates the gate and fence.)* Now you can go in.

Auxiliaries
These are members of the group who play minor parts in the psychodrama. In Moreno's theater they are professionals.

Auxiliaries Come into Play
In this example the auxiliaries are children chosen by the protagonist at the suggestion of the director.

Billy: Mrs. David was cross because . . .
Director: We need someone to be Mrs. David. Who do you think, Billy?
Billy: Janie.
Director: You try being Mrs. David, Janie. (Janie takes up a position on "stage.") What does she say, Billy?

Role Reversal
This is a technique by which the protagonist and auxiliary change roles. The protagonist may feel that the auxiliary is not playing her part accurately, and the director suggests the protagonist demonstrate it. Alternatively, the director may decide to use the technique because she feels that the protagonist could profit from seeing the situation from another point of view.

Janie: *(as Mrs. David)* You're a very naughty boy.
Billy: But she didn't say that.
Director: You try being Mrs. David, Billy, and show us what she said. Janie, you be Billy. Go on Billy, what did she say?

The Mirror Technique

This is a technique by which the protagonist sees her behavior imitated by an auxiliary.

Billy: Yes, Mrs. David *(he goes out and shuts the gate).*
Director: Will someone do what Billy just did? Sam?
(Sam repeats the performance, exaggerating Billy's look of defiance as he slams the gate.)
Director: Did Billy really look like that? . . . What do you think, Billy?

Doubling

An auxiliary stands behind, or at the side of the protagonist and serves as the "alter ego."

(Billy slams the gate.)
Director: (to group) How do you think Billy felt when he did that? *(The children start to speak up.)*
Director: Yvonne, you stand beside Billy, and when he slams the gate, you slam the gate and say what you think Billy wants to say, but doesn't.
(Billy and Yvonne slam the gate.)
Yvonne: I hate you and I wish you'd die!

The Empty Chair

The director places an empty chair on stage. She says that the chair represents Mrs. David and invites the children to approach it and speak to it any way they wish. Out of this may come the opportunity for further exploration, perhaps through giving the children the opportunity to express their frustration at the unreasonable behavior of adults. (pp. 196–97)

The teacher or director may not use all the techniques described above. The main focus should be to give the student, in this case Billy, as much control in exploring the situation. The teacher is not concerned here with how good an actor the student is but in exploring the feelings, reactions, and attitudes of those involved in the drama, particularly the protagonist (e.g., Billy). Neville suggests that "for children, an activity like this is very natural, not far removed from their spontaneous play" (p. 198). Moreno, in fact, called his approach the Theater of Spontaneity.

Moreno felt that adults, particularly, can become frozen in their behavior and roles. In order to break away from these scripts he focused on improvisation that focuses on our feelings in the here and now. If we can focus more on the here and now we can give up the "frozen roles" and "feel our energy flowing out into behavior which is new and adaptable and creative" (p. 200). Young children tend to be naturally spontaneous, but as they get older pressure from both the school and peers forces the student into more constricted and frozen patterns of behavior. Neville argues that we need a Dionysian schooling that nourishes the child's soul through "play, dance, and drama" (p. 201). Dionysus was the Greek of emotional release but a release "crafted with intelligence and sensitivity into a work of art which would engage and entrance and transport an audience" (p. 201).

The teacher needs to develop a climate in the classroom where students can act spontaneously and naturally. If the teacher wants students to explore a specific topic, he or she can provides a warm-up by telling a story that is related to the subject to be explored in the drama. After telling the story, there then can be time for questions or sometimes a short time for meditation or silence that provide a transition to the drama itself. Another warm-up activity can be a simple game that loosens up the students so that they enter the role-playing relaxed and uninhibited.

Neville suggests that if you are directing a drama based on an incident related to a particular student it is easier to construct the drama with that student as a witness who helps direct the drama and explore possible solutions. Sometimes this is called playback:

> Rebecca tells her story and a group of students immediately act it out, without rehearsal and after only a few moments of preparation. If Rebecca finds that the performance does not give an accurate picture of her experience she can explain what is lacking and the actors can repeat the performance. Playback is an ideal instrument for developing intuition and spontaneity while focusing on a task. (p. 206)

Another technique is for the student to describe the situation to be enacted and then the class can be broken into a pairs or triads to act it out. Neville argues that the experience should be enjoyable for both the teacher and the student. To facilitate this process he asks the following questions:

> How can I make this learning enjoyable for the students? but also, How can I engage in this topic in a way which calls on all of my imagination, skills, and quick wittedness, as well as those of my students? How can I craft this lesson into an original work of art? How can I be with my students so completely in this lesson that we really experience something new together? (p. 209)

Neville describes how drama can be used within different subject areas. For example, in studying the French Revolution, the teacher could have a student take on the role of Marie Antoinette and her attempted flight from France and have the student describe her hopes, fears, and fantasies. The teacher could also have two chairs facing each other so that the students could role-play Robespierre and Danton debating each other. Two students could take these roles, or the chairs could be left open and students could sit in them when they want to contribute to the debate.

In language class, the students can take on the role of the author or one of the characters in a novel. Students, for example, might play the role of Anna Karenina and describe her feelings and why she had become so unhappy.

In science the teacher can designate a key word and then have students mime the meaning of the word. For example, the student can mime such concepts as photosynthesis, osmosis, and erosion. Another mime involves the student taking on the role of a particular atom and bonding with other atoms to form molecules. This encourages the student to express concepts in a nonverbal manner and to use their imagination and intuition.

As mentioned earlier the goal in psychodrama is to facilitate a spontaneity that is both freeing and nourishing for the soul. Neville summarizes: "Our godlikeness is our spontaneity and spontaneity involves doing something new and is always opposed to the cultural conserve" (p. 214).

CREATIVE WRITING/POETRY

Another way to nourish the soul is through creative writing. One of the best examples of how this can be done is through the work of Phillip Lopate (1975). Lopate, a poet and writer, worked in an elementary school (P.S. 90) in New York City and used writing to stimulate the student's creative voice. Lopate wanted his students to avoid gimmicks and techniques. For example he found that students often end a story suddenly with something like "And then I woke up and it was all a dream" (p. 272). Lopate says:

> I wondered if there was a way to lead children slowly into a writing that had no compulsory ending. To connect them with processes and flows that were ongoing, infinite. Their panic before the Infinite was very real; I had it myself. Yet the only way to write good modern poetry, or the sort I like, Open Poetry, was to take the voyage into openness and to discover the poem in the act of writing it. (p. 273)

Lopate started by having students assume roles (e.g., an old woman, a policeman, etc.) and then write one or two lines expressing the viewpoint of this individual. Next he asked them to just write for ten minutes everything that came into their heads. One student, Xiomara, wrote about the other students and seemed to take responsibility for their behavior. Lopate called her the "self-appointed den mother of the class." Other students became quite personal in their statements as some talked about dying while others expressed their dislike of school and even themselves (e.g., "I hate myself").

Next Lopate had the students do an exercise where they feigned madness and then wrote about the experience. He had students first walk in normal manner and then for a moment do something abnormal. After this experience, one student wrote this:

> With an open eye nothing can be seen. But with the closed eye the entire world is open to you. With the open eye, death, destruction and poverty, with the closed eye, life, serenity and Eden. (p. 286)

Next, he took the students outside and had them write down their impressions of what they saw on the streets of New York. Then he had them connect what they saw outside to their inner life. Lopate found that the second step was more difficult than just recording their impressions of street life.

The next exercise began with students listening sensitively to conversations going on in the school and then write them up in some form. The kids loved this exercise although Lopate found that it did not stimulate as much insight as some of the other activities he gave the children. Consistent among the exercises was the intent to get the students to see things in a clear way. In another exercise, the students wrote portraits of their teachers. He found that some students were able to catch the rhythm and cadence of the teacher they were observing. Lopate comments on one student's (Eve) writing about her teacher Miss Mayer:

> What impressed me so much was that the portrait was neither adulatory nor insulting, but clear-eyed. The rhythm and tracking speed of Eve's prose seemed to bring Miss Mayer's movements alive. (p. 317)

In the last lesson Lopate asked them to write about the history of a friendship or in some cases "enemyship" (a word developed for this project). Again he was pleased with results as "all of the papers had an honesty that gave privileged glimpses of that mysterious subcontinent of children's friendships" (p. 321).

In summarizing his work Lopate suggests that through the project students began to see the world around them more clearly and were able to describe it in a nonjudgmental way. At the same time, the creative writing allowed the students to express their feelings. In each case, the child's soul was nourished through reflection and from bringing intuitively grasped truths into conscious expression.

MUSIC

I have already referred to music and the soul when I discussed the work of Plato. The ancients believed that music could help align the soul with the music of the spheres and the universe. Even today we recognize the healing power of music when we hear or play it. Consider the words of Mildred Portney Chase (1974), a pianist.

> I am now able to reach a state of being at the piano from which I come away renewed and at peace with myself, having established a harmony of the mind, heart, and body. This does not diminish my performance in any way, either in style or communicativeness. In fact, it is quite the opposite. The heightened awareness and the sense of harmony that I take away with me from the instrument benefit the people with whom I interact, and the other activities that occupy me. We bring to our music from our lives and take from our music to the rest of our living. (p. 3)

> With the piano, body movement always plays a part. You need to move in order to create the sound. A feeling of oneness with the instrument is an ultimate requirement. This will express itself in beautiful movement, that is, coordination, and will represent a state of harmony within the person. (p. 9)

Sandra Reid (1995) argues that music is a subject that can be integrated with other subjects and also enhance the student's personal development. For example, in studying the history or geography of a country the students can listen to the music of that country. Students can also listen to and sing the folk songs of the country that they are studying. In language class students can listen to music and then write in their journals. Sometimes novels make reference to music and the music referred to can be played and listened to.

There are also many natural connections between math and music. Reid suggests:

Sing the multiplication tables in *Don't Want Your Weavily Wheat* (Musi-canda 5) or have students make up a rap with a prerecorded rhythm for memorizing facts. Look at half-tones and whole tones and patterns for scales. Chart and graph favorite pieces or performing groups. (p. 12)

Reid (in press) also makes reference to the work of Zoltan Kodaly, which can be used to integrate music into the curriculum. Kodaly felt that music should be studied in relation to the cultural context from which the music is derived. Kodaly believed that music education can begin with the child's own voice and mother tongue.

In this context Reid (1990) argues that children's singing games can be taught to students. This form of music goes back to indigenous peoples' cultures where "Indian tribes in North America—the Chipewa, Yuma, Makah, Ute, and Hopi tribes had children's songs for the purpose of teaching the young to do essential tasks through games" (p. 13). Singing songs from different periods of history can help in understanding the culture of that period. For example the song "How Many Miles to Babylon" refers to the custom of charging a toll on merchandise entering a walled town. The song "Old Roger is dead, Old Roger is dead. They planted an apple tree over his head" refers to the custom of planting a tree at the head or foot of the grave because people believed that the soul of the dead person went into the tree.

Songs have been used by cultures to transmit customs and values. In the Jewish tradition the mother's lullabies stress cultural values such as "Sleep soundly by night and learn Torah by day, And thou'lt be a rabbi when I have grown gray." Swaying as one sings is also important within this tradition.

Reid (1991) suggests that movement is often integral to children's singing:

> When children perform their own songs they never stand still. The movements they use demand considerable coordination and skill. . . . It is interesting to note that the singing and movement are so closely intertwined that in trying to recall game songs both adults and children automatically start the actions with the song. (p. 14)

Another approach to music education that I would like to mention here is Education Through Music (ETM), which Campbell and Scott-Kassner (1995) refer to as "a holistic approach to music instruction" (p. 62). This approach was developed by Mary

Helen Richards who was influenced by Kodaly. She developed a program based, in part, on North American and British folk songs. ETM uses a lot of group singing that also includes a wide variety of movement activities.

It is beyond the scope of this section to discuss other forms of music education. Also I have not been able to deal with all of the arts in the chapter. For example I have not included dance and movement education; however, please see *The Holistic Curriculum* (pp. 113–20) where I discuss movement, dance, and eurythmy.

INTEGRATING SUBJECTS THROUGH THE ARTS

Merryl Goldberg (1997) argues that diffcrent subjects can be learned *with* and *through* the arts. For example she gives examples of how science can be taught with the help of the arts. She suggests that student could go to a museum and look at the landscape paintings and explore questions such as "How would you describe the weather in the different paintings? Can you predict the weather? What are your clues. What kind of clouds are depicted? What elements of nature are shown in each painting?" (p. 106). Music can also be used in the same way since there are many musical pieces that depict scenes in nature. Students could listen to Debussy's *La Mer* and describe how they feel this music represents the sea. Goldberg lists some other pieces that could link music to science:

> Grofe: *Grand Canyon Suite*
> Holst: *The Planets*
> Rimsky-Korsakov: *The Flight of the Bumblebee*
> Stravinsky: *The Rite of Spring*
> Vivaldi: *The Four Seasons*

(p. 107)

Dance and movement can also be used to explore issues in science. If the students were studying the concept of chaos the "teacher might have the students move throughout a room without touching each other. . . . To explore life cycles, have them dramatize the events of a metamorphosis. Have them act out the life of a butterfly from pupa to full-grown butterfly, or the life cycle of a tornado" (p. 108).

Goldberg makes the point that drawing has always been a tool of the naturalist. So a unit on science could have the students sketch "leaves, shells, flowers, seaweed, and so on" (p. 109). In drawing the object the student becomes an active observer of nature. As the student draws the tree or leaf he or she may want to inquire deeper into the nature of the object being drawn. Goldberg cites the work of Margot Grallert (1991) who suggests that students draw an object from inside out rather than starting with the border.

Goldberg states that as the student sketches the object the student makes two lists. One list includes a set of questions about the object and the other list includes things that the students notices about the object.

> They often note interesting things about their shell such as the amount of lines in its curved shape, the detail in the patterns, and shapes on the shell. They may begin to wonder: What is the shell made of? Does it grow? Did anything live in this shell? Where is it now? How did it get out? How did the shell end up on the beach? Was it out very far in the ocean? Did it travel from somewhere else to get here? Did the waves push it? How far? These and other questions that arise from the graphic exercise form the basis for the science lessons. (p. 111)

Another teacher had students draw a chrysanthemum flower. Drawing the flower led to the following questions.

> Why are leaves in different shapes?
> Why do flowers have leaves?
> What kind of flower did we draw?
> Why are stems green?
> Why do flowers smell?
> What do plants make for us?
> How do plants make their food?
> Why do some plants have thorns?
> Why are there so many different plants?
> Why are they all colors?
> Who names flowers?
> How do you know what flower it is?
> Why do they need soil, water, air?
>
> (p. 111)

Goldberg makes a strong case for how the arts can also be used to stimulate learning in other subjects including social studies, language and even math.

FINAL THOUGHTS

Again the teacher's presence and commitment are fundamental to arts education. Of course, we cannot expect the teacher to be an expert artist but the teacher should be able to take risks in trying out various artistic activities and perhaps at least develop some skills in one of the arts. By studying one of the arts' and feeling its effect on his or her own soul, the teacher can then imagine the arts impact on the student's soul.

Waldorf education is a wonderful example of how the arts can be integrated into the life of the classroom. I believe that public school educators can learn from Waldorf schools and adapt some of the Steiner approaches to the public school classroom. For example, teacher education in the Waldorf puts a strong emphasis on the arts so that teachers at all levels can integrate arts into the subject matter. I remember going into a science class in a Waldorf high school and seeing beautiful pictures of various atomic structures on the board that had been drawn by the teacher. When the arts have been integrated into the life of the classroom in this way the children's souls are nourished.

6

Earth and the Soul

Our souls need a sense of place. We often experience soul in nature because the direct experience of the sun, trees, grass, flowers, and the earth is so nourishing to our soul. I prefer the term *earth education* rather than *environmental education* for this reason. The word *earth* gives me more of a sense of place than *environment*. I can feel and touch the earth and there is both reverence and sensuality in this experience.

When I am truly present in nature I feel a sense of awe and reverence from just witnessing the beauty of it all. At the same time seeing the colors of the flowers, the blue sky, and feeling the grass under my bare feet are sensuous experiences. Both the reverence and sensuality nourish soul. As recently as the nineteenth century, our culture recognized the ennobling work of nature upon the soul as evidenced in the work of Frederick Law Olmstead, a great designer of public spaces, the most famous of them being Central Park in New York. Governments then were eager to commission Olmstead to create beautiful public spaces because we had not yet lost sight of the connection between nature and the health of the soul.

Thomas Moore comments how two chestnut trees in front of his great grandparents' house had a strong impact on his soul. When he visited the old homestead, the barn had collapsed and grass had grown around the house's foundation. But the trees were still there and had "not lost their nobility and kindliness" (p. 402). Moore recalls how people had sat under those trees and told stories to each other. Moore advocates a "soul-ecology" where we respect the soul in nature that is based on a "felt relationship." He argues that the root meaning of ecology is seeing the Earth as "home." We are moved to take care of earth as we would our own home when we feel a deep affection for it.

Moore goes on to suggest that the problem of what he refers to as our homelessness is rooted in our abstraction from the earth. Because we have lost the felt relationship to the Earth most human beings have become inwardly homeless on the planet. The Zuni Indians of New Mexico see their home as a "particular place and the entire world." It is possible, then, to see our homes as places where our individual souls connect to the world soul.

Earth education should have as its ultimate reference point the cosmos itself. This is the most inclusive context for studying the earth as Moffett (1994) has described in his work. In contrast, the most frequent reference point for education is the globally competitive economy for which we must prepare our children. Instead of educating human beings, we are asked to only train workers. Thomas Merton once called this whole process, "the mass production of people literally unfit for anything except to take part in an elaborate and completely artificial charade." (p. 154)

Earth education must not be limited to one subject in the curriculum. In fact, it could a unifying theme for the whole curriculum. Swimme and Berry (1992) make a compelling argument for this in what they call the Universe Story.

> Education might well be defined as knowing the story of the universe, of the planet Earth, of life systems, and of consciousness, all as a single story, and recognizing the human role in the story. The primary purpose of education should be to enable individual humans to fulfill their proper role in their larger pattern of meaning. We can understand this role in the Great Story only if we know the story in its full dimensions (p. 256)

Almost everything in the curriculum could be included in the Universe Story as all subject matter could be woven around this story. Swimme and Berry (1992) believe that the story is a means by which the educator can transcend the science/humanities division in the curriculum:

> It is our hope that this story will provide a new unity to the educational process from its earliest beginnings through the highest level of training in the various professions. In this manner all the professions and institutions of our culture might be renewed. (p. 5)

The story is a unique combination of scientific knowledge and soul both individual and world.

Earth education demands that things and events be looked within larger patterns and relationships. David Orr (1994) suggests that many of our personal and societal problems stem from seeing the world in a fragmented and disconnected way. Building freeways, shopping malls, parking lots at a nonstop pace without consideration of the real need and impact on ecology is a product of the compartmentalized way of seeing and behaving.

> These things are threads of a whole cloth. The fact that we see them as disconnected events or fail to see them at all is, I believe, evidence of a considerable failure that we have yet to acknowledge as an educational failure. It is a failure to educate people to think broadly, to perceive systems and patterns and to live as whole persons. (p. 2)

John Ralston Saul in his 1995 Massey Lectures, *The Unconscious Civilization* points out the failure to make important connections in our society. In one ecological example, he states:

> The world-wide depletion of fish stocks is a recent example. The number of fish caught between 1950 and 1989 multiplied by five. The fishing fleet went from 585,000 boats in 1970 to 1.2 million boats in 1990 and on to 3.5 million today. No one thought about the long- or even the medium-term maintenance of stocks; not the fishermen, not the boat builders, not the fish wholesalers, who found new uses for their product, including fertilizer and chicken feed; not the financiers. It wasn't their job. Their job was to worry about their own interests. (p. 135)

As we awaken to the Earth and its processes, we free ourselves from this modern blindness and start to look at life interdependently. We then can see the effects of industrialization in the air we breathe and the water we drink, not to the mention the harm to the ozone layer and the ongoing process of global warming. A strictly rationalist approach to life denies this broader perspective. A soulful approach not only enables but demands such a perspective because soul is immersed in connections.

Education that is sensitive to earth and soul must be authentic because as students necessarily gain in awareness, false notes from educators will become very apparent. Teachers and administrators must carry this sensitivity into their work and life so that students see living examples of this sensitivity and so learn to trust both the message and messengers. In chapter 8, I discuss ways in which teachers can work on themselves to bring this deeper sensitivity into their lives.

In chapter 7, I also discuss the means by which we can bring soul into the school. For example, making the school a more beautiful place is one way that we can do this. By bringing plants and art into the school and taking care of these objects in a caring way, we begin to demonstrate a sense of reverence.

Earth education can, as a starting point, ask students to investigate the kind world they live in. For example, they can pursue the following questions:

- What soil series are you standing on?
- When was the last time a fire burned in your area?
- Name five native edible plants in your region and their seasons of availability.
- From what direction do winter storms generally come in your region?
- Where does your garbage go?
- How long is the growing season where you live?
- Name five grasses in your area. Are any of them native?
- Name five resident and five migratory birds in your area.
- What primary geological event or processes influenced the land from where you live?
- What species have become extinct in your area?
- What are the major plant associations in your region ?

(*Co-Evolution Quarterly* 32 [Winter 1981–82]: 1)

Although these kinds of questions are helpful, earth education is at its best when encountered within a total school environment that is committed to this form of learning. I now describe two examples of schools where the Earth is at the center of the curriculum.

OJIYA SCHOOL

When I was in Japan in 1994 I had the opportunity to visit a school that demonstrated the sense of caring and reverence to which I have referred at the beginning of this chapter. Ojiya school is described in detail by Ikue Tezuka (1995) in a book entitled *School with Forest and Meadow*.

This school is fortunate to be situated on large grounds. The school itself is rectangular and encircles an open area that is called the Friendship Pasture. Living in this pasture are a variety of animals including goats, chickens, rabbits, and turtles. The pasture is a 440 square meter pen surrounded by a net that was made with the help of parents and teachers. When the weather is good the animals are let out to feed on the grounds. The children love to go into the pasture to "touch, hold, speak to, and take care of the animals" (p. 3). Tezuka, who has visited the school on several occasions writes "One can observe the children growing in love and gentleness through taking care of their animal friends" (p. 4). When I walked into the pasture during my visit, my first impression was of three boys on a bench each holding and petting a rabbit, confirming Tezuka's remarks.

Tezuka reports that, at first, many children were afraid of the animals. Many students did not like the chickens, which they felt were dirty and smelled bad. But gradually they began to change in their attitude on closer acquaintance. "Now the children run to the pens and buildings at cleaning time in the morning. They look forward to taking care of the rabbits. They even like to clean the hen house" (p. 5). The students have come "to sympathize with these creatures and sense their own kinship with them" (p. 6).

The school also has a small forest called "Yasho Homeland Forest" with about three hundred trees. Before the students and teachers planted the trees, they surveyed the surrounding area and identified all the different kinds of native trees. They found ninety-six different kinds of trees and shrubs within ten kilometers of the school. In planting the trees, attention was given to the size and colors of the flowers and buds, incorporating consideration of aesthetic principles into the learning of natural science. Tezuka describes the result:

> The result is beautiful to see. Spring is the season of the biggest change. Many of the trees burst forth in buds and blossoms at the same time. In May, the green grows deeper and the red blossoms are brilliant against the green background. The red azaleas are especially beautiful. From early summer to autumn, the various trees flower one after another with their white, red, and purple flowers. In autumn, the trees bend toward the earth under their load of delicious fruit. Then comes the season of autumnal coloring. Red and yellow leaves are beautiful against the background of the evergreen. The leaves of deciduous trees begin to fall, covering the ground like a beautiful carpet. In winter, the trees stand silent, waiting for the thaw which will bring them back to life. Some begin to flower in the snow. (p. 10)

The students are very concerned about the trees. If there is a typhoon, the first thing they do is look at the trees to see if they are all right when they come the next day. The students write about their feelings for the trees in poems,

Trees in the Home Forest
by Yukari Kazama

I saw trees in the ground.
They are moving as if they were dancing with snow.
Don't they feel heavy
When they have snow on their branches!

Trees
by Takumi Yokota

I saw trees.
They look as if they were weeping in the snow.
Don't they feel pain when they are bound with ropes?
I'd like to remove the ropes to make then feel better.

Home Forest
by Rie Sato

Trees in Home Forest.
Dead Trees.
They are covered with snow.
They look as if they were saying, "It's cold."
They seem to be saying to the neighboring trees:
"It's cold. I hope spring comes soon."
The trees are good friends.

(p. 10–11)

The poems are evidence that children at Ojiya School are learning a deep reverence for the natural world. They are also gaining in their knowledge of the principles of conservation as they progress with their care of the trees. For example, when fall came, they used to put the fallen leaves in a bag for disposal and now they put the leaves under the trees to help enrich the soil there.

The person responsible for the approach at Ojiya School is Giichiro Yamanouchi, a former principal. He felt that a forest could provide many learning opportunities for children and also foster their ability to take care of the natural environment around them. He also believed that it would be useful for learning science and writing compositions as well as other learning activities. He thinks that the forest is also good for the children's souls. Once he talked to the children of another school—Kawasaki School—where they had built a forest. Yamanouchi said:

You go to the forest often, don't you? When you come to school in the morning, at break times, and after school, I am glad. Some people believe that the forest is sacred, and when you go into it you can be your true self. Forests are natural meditation rooms where we can be alone and listen quietly to the forest. This helps our souls to grow strong. There is good, clean air, in the forest also, which is good for our bodies. If we are troubled in body and or in our minds, we can go into the forest to meditate and to breathe deeply and we can become renewed and vigorous. (p. 56)

The forest also stimulates self-directed learning activity. One child who had never made any initiative on his own became more alert and wrote a five-page composition about the forest. Another child became more observant of birds in the area as a result of the forest.

Birds and the Protection of Nature
by Takeshi Morohashi

Isn't nature the most important thing for us? But if it is being lost, how can we learn about it? From newspapers? On TV? These tell us about the destruction of nature as news, after it happens. Then it is almost too late to do anything. Isn't there some way in which we can learn about these things sooner, before nature is destroyed? One way that I thought of was to observe living creatures because they are nature itself. So I began to observe birds as a kind of "barometer." I compared the numbers and kinds of birds I observed in three areas in Nagaoka city: in front of the station, around this school and on the Shinano river.

There were only 5 species in front of the station; dove, starling, swallow, sparrow, and crow. Around the school, I observed 23 species and on the Shinano River there were 33 different kinds of birds: 6 species of heron, 13 of duck and goose, 7 of eagle and hawk, and 7 of snipe. There is a big difference in the number of species in the 3 places.

I compared not only the number but the nature of the birds. In front of the station, there were only birds which can live in crowded, noisy places. Around the school, there were birds which do not like noisy places and can live only in residential areas. If the whole of Nagaoka city becomes like the area around the station, what will happen to the birds?

Then, how about planting more trees like Kawasaki Forest? Birds will surely be attracted to them. Planting trees helps to protect nature. The protection of nature is not only monitoring national parks but also doing more common things such as making a wooden path in Kawasaki Forest, studying about trees in it, taking care of them, and not filling the Suyoshi River with dirty water. We should develop this kind of attitude if we want to protect nature. (pp. 60–61)

I find this such an interesting example of earth education because the student initiated his own investigation. Clearly this student is learning reverence for the natural world and is taking some form of action to preserve it.

Parents also became convinced of the value of the forest project. Their enthusiasm prompted them to help raise money for the forest. In all the schools where he has served as principal, Yamanouchi worked with parents and community members to help the school. One of his schools was located in a community where raising carp was a local industry. He was able to persuade a person who raised the expensive fish to donate some to the school. The children again learned how to take care of these fish and the donation of the fish created a lot of community interest in the school.

Yamanouchi also believes in what he calls *integrated learning activity*. He objects to textbook learning that is so common in Japan. Instead, he feels learning activities should be connected to the interests of the students. He explains:

> Thus, in integrated activity, we connect the curriculum to carp-raising and we say, "Let's raise carp as good as your fathers do!" Then they will be excited and eager to learn about science. . . . Unless we connect the curriculum to producing something, the children's interest and imagination will not be activated and they cannot learn. The main contribution we as teachers can make to children's learning is to make them excited and impressed with something. Such integrated experiences provide a base for comprehending science, arithmetic, language, etc. This kind of learning experience nurtures and enhances a child's ability to engage in abstract thinking.
>
> The most important responsibility of teachers is to help children grow to be a human being, having much knowledge is not important. To think for oneself, to learn independently, to treat others kindly and fairly to work with friends, to encourage others, to say what one thinks, and to act as one thinks: these are the things which are important. And, of course, a strong, healthy body is also important. In other words, a child needs help in developing all aspects of her personality and her life as a human being. (pp. 44–45)

I have met and worked with Yamanouchi and he is one of the most interesting and passionate educators I have ever met. Although he is retired now, he is still very active and extremely energetic. He is also president of the Japanese Holistic Education Society and is doing much to bring holistic education into the public schools in Japan.

An example of the type of integrated activities that he encouraged in one of the schools can be seen below.

1st graders:
- making masks of leaves;
- making dolls of pampas grass and corn;
- going to the house of an elderly woman to listen to folk tales and folklore.

2nd graders:
- dyeing with grass and wood;
- making picture books.

3rd graders:
- raising silkworms, making silk, and weaving cloth;
- researching new year's customs and events;
- praying for a rich harvest.

4th graders:
- raising buckwheat from sowing to harvesting
- making noodles from the buckwheat and eating them.

5th graders:
- planting and raising rice
- harvesting, drying, and threshing rice;
- raising red beans
- making rice cakes.

(pp. 46–7)

Tezuka, in concluding her book comments on Yamanouchi's work: "Through the work of such dedicated people as Giichiro Yamanouchi, amazing things are beginning to happen. . . . There is developing a ground swell movement toward holistic student-centered education in our country (p. 88).

Oijya School for me is a place that nourishes the student's soul by the connections that are made to all forms of life. Students relate deeply to the plants, animals, and trees that are part of the fabric of the school.

THE BLACK ROCK FOREST PROJECT

In 1991, teachers and administrators from the Newburgh Enlarged City School District, met in Newburgh, New York, to address this question: "We have access to 3,700 acres of protected ponds, streams and woodlands. How should use we them?" (Murray 1993, p. 44). The Newburgh Enlarged City School District is about fifty miles north of New York City and contains eleven elementary schools, a middle school, two junior high schools, and one high school.

In describing the project, Murray (1993) quotes Allan Gussow's following remarks, which are very relevant to the theme of this chapter.

> There is a great deal of talk these days about saving the environment. We must, for the environment sustains our bodies. But as humans we also require support for our spirits, and this is what certain places provide. The catalyst that converts any physical location—any environment if you will—into a place, is the process of experiencing deeply. A place is a piece of the whole environment that has been claimed by feeling. (p. 46).

The project developed a number of goals but central to the project, was developing in students, a sense of "awe, wonder, reverence, and respect" (p. 46) So the teachers and individuals tried to instill in students a sense of place that is also "claimed by feeling." Four schools from the district were involved in the project and each used the area in a different way. One school, the Magnet Middle School, had seventh-graders go into the forest every day for seven weeks.

Between April and June, twenty-four students experienced a totally integrated learning experience that was developed and guided by middle school staff. Students worked in groups of eight during the project. Groups were able to initiate their own learning projects. Students not only learned skills and knowledge related to the environment, their journals also revealed the impact of the project on their emotional development. One student commented on her experiences in an interesting way:

> The beautiful world of fish and water creatures
> While the wind blows on my face.
> I feel the love and tenderness of the human race.
> If I could jump in the air and glide like a bird in the sky

I would love it.
The two islands are the two eyes on my face.
The water is my blood flowing freely in my body.
And the trees are my hair
Grown freely without despair.
Last of all, the land is my beautiful skin like a round ball.
Now you know what Tamarack means to me.
—Lemont Collins, Magnet Middle School student (p. 47)

The students in the middle school also "buddied up" with students from the primary school while they were in the forest. The older students were put into a responsible adult role of having to look after a younger person. Students commented in their journals about the importance of this experience and how they felt close to the younger students.

Parents who were involved in the project were deeply affected.

I grew up around Black Rock Forest and have long been a member of the Black Rock Fish and Game Club. I thought that I knew the forest like the back of my hand. Seeing it through the eyes of my five-year-old daughter changed my mind. I now look at it with awe and wonder, and I can't wait to go back. I'm seeing it through the eyes of a child for the first time. (p. 54)

When a project instills this kind of wonder in an adult then I think we can call it a soulful project. Listen also to the words of two seventh graders involved in the project who wrote: "The world is awake, the sunrise sparkles loudly; how peaceful, how bold" (p. 55).

EARTH LITERATURE

Many students do not have access to woodland like Black Rock Forest, so we must attempt to bring a sense of the Earth into the school. As I mentioned earlier, this can be done by bringing plants and animals into the school. Another useful technique is to read indigenous people's literature. Once I went into a Catholic elementary school and students sat in a circle each morning. In the middle of the circle was the Bible as well as a book called *Earth Prayers* (Roberts and Amidon). When the students met in the circle they would often read from both books. Below is an Ojibway prayer from this book.

Grandfather,
Look at our brokeness.

We know that in all creation
Only the human family
Has strayed from the Sacred Way.

We know that we are the ones
Who are divided.
And we are the ones
Who must come back together
To walk in the Sacred Way.

Grandfather,
Sacred one,
Teach us love, compassion, and honor
That we may heal the earth
and heal each other. (p. 95)

Another helpful book is *Touch the Earth* (McLuhan 1972).

Hills are always more beautiful than stone buildings, you know. Living in a city is an artificial existence. Lots of people hardly feel real soil under their feet, see plants grow except in flower pots, or get far enough beyond the street light to catch the enchantment of a night sky studded with stars. When people live far from scenes of the Great Spirit's making, it's easy for them to forget his laws.

We saw the Great Spirit's work in almost everything: sun, moon, trees, wind, and mountains. Sometimes we approached him through these things. Was that so bad? I think we have a true belief in the supreme being, a stronger faith than that of most whites who have called us pagans. . . . Indians living close to nature and nature's ruler are not living in darkness. Did you know that trees talk: Well they do. They talk each other, and they'll talk to you if you listen. Trouble is, white people don't listen. They never learned to listen to the Indians so I don't suppose they'll listen to other voices in nature. But I have learned a lot from trees; sometimes about the weather, sometimes about animals, sometimes about the Great Spirit. (p. 230)

—Walking Buffalo

The children at Ojiya School learned to connect to trees in the way Walking Buffalo suggests.

EARTH ACTIVITIES

Twenty-five years ago, a colleague of mine moved his family from the city to a rural property in Northern Ontario. Over time, this family discovered deeply satisfying ways of engaging their environment. Now, as a guide to grandchildren and others who will follow, these activities have been formed into a hierarchy (Robinson 1998). I include a description of them here because I believe that teachers and parents interested in earth education would benefit greatly from exploring these activities.

The first level of activities includes sensual contact with the four basic earth elements (and other aspects of nature): i) getting your hands or feet in the earth, or in sand; ii) making a wood (and sometimes grass) fire and letting the smoke waft over you; iii) listening to, and putting your feet in water (especially running water); iv) sitting still and soaking up heat from the winter or early spring sun; v) walking in the rain; vi) listening to the wind in the trees, and feeling it blow against your face, and vii) sitting on, and running your hands over, ancient rocks; viii) experiencing a sense of wonder when looking at the Milky Way or displays of Northern Lights: ix) experiencing the near absolute silence of a winter night in a remote place; x) eating berries from the vine, or vegetables fresh from the garden. There is a meditative quality to all of these activities.

The second level includes caring engagement with plants and animals i) locating, and observing with awe and reverence, rare or exceptional species; ii) studying the interaction among and between different species (e.g., birds), iii) planting and caring for a vegetable garden; iv) caring for a "pet" (any kind of animal) through its life cycle; v) responding to crises/catastrophes in the plant and animal worlds (e.g. feeding deer in exceptionally harsh winters).

The third level includes interacting positively with ecosystems: i) regulating water flows to increase their water holding potential, and the complexity of their associated ecosystems; ii) increasing the biological diversity of an area by cautiously importing new species; iii) harvesting wild vegetables and fruits; iv) healing denuded land by reforesting; v) tracing waterways to their source; vi) making "least invasive" walking trails to otherwise inaccessible places; vii) tracking animals for the purpose of understanding their movements, and getting to witness their passing; viii) "making friends with" animals by imitating their sounds to bring them closer, then engaging in voiceless, mutual contemplation; ix) sustaining oneself in the wild (eating, sleeping outside with the least possible dependence on man-made things). By gradually building up a deeper and more extensive understanding of the surrounding ecosystems and one's sense of connection with these systems helps intensify our connection to the World Soul as described by Sardello.

At the next level children can create and walk paths and trails that have symbolic, ritual, and meditative functions: i) discovering and re-opening abandoned (pioneer) trials; ii) making walking paths to very remote places; and iii) constructing labyrinths.

At the last level children can become conscious of the present place and moment as an event in the Great Story. On our property this can begin by sitting on a high, bare (600 million year old) rock ridge that overlooks our valley and predates all its life forms. Here the person can visualize the gradual evolution of the land forms and plant and animal species of increasing complexity as well as the aboriginal peoples living there. Settlers cleared the arable land about a century ago, and artifacts of their habitation, work, and life style are still visible. (Robinson 1998)

Today the story continues to evolve and Floyd Robinson and his family see themselves having some role in shaping the future. He states "In our imagination, the interaction between future residents and the natural world continues to become more sustained and mutually beneficial. Also we continue to see our property as connected to larger and larger systems so that co-planning with neighbors with regard to shared trails and co-conservation projects seems an obvious task for the next generation."

I believe that Floyd Robinson has identified a number of interesting ways to help awaken in ourselves and in our students what Emerson called our "original relationship to the universe." As parents, teachers, and children engage in these activities they can begin to see theworld with fresh eyes. At the same time the soul is also nourished through this connection with the earth.

FINAL THOUGHTS

The students will be looking to the teachers and how they care for the Earth. They will notice if the teachers do not treat the environment with respect and reverence. We can hardly ask students to be sensitive to the Earth if we ignore or abuse it. This is more than reusing and recycling material; it is seeing that we are part of the Earth and what native peoples call the "web of life." Our sensitivity to this interdependence should permeate everything that occurs within the classroom and the school.

7

The Soulful School

The school itself also has a soul; however, this is rarely acknowledged. Instead, schools tend be seen as machines or factories. An
example of this approach is the importing of principles and language from the business world's "Total Quality Management"
(TQM) movement. Management is seen as a linear process that
includes mathematical models, "measurement controls, process
controls, statistical analysis, data collection tools, cybernetic systems, and feedback loops" (Secretan 1996, p. 17). Sometimes institutions and schools are "reengineered" to make "leaner and
meaner" units. There is little room for soul in an institution that has
been reengineered. The result of these activities is what Dalla Costa
(1995) calls "change fatigue" (p. 10). Referring to industry, Dalla
Costa (1995) gives some examples of change fatigue:

> Employees read the new corporate mission, attend its launch meet-
> ing, or see the explanatory video, and still walk away lethargic, unin-
> spired, or even ashen. In subsequent meetings, they will say things
> like: "We need to wait until the mission is worked out."
>
> Throughout the company individuals use the language of change
> like real pros, with the facility of the consultant who introduced it
> into the corporate culture, but without meaning a word of it. It is not
> for lack of trying. They have mastered the vocabulary because they
> know it is important, but no one was there to help them through the
> mess of implementation, so for the sake of getting things done they
> resort to old practices. . . .
>
> Senior management and employees come to value the opinion of
> an outside change specialist more than any opinion generated inter-
> nally. This continuous seeking of a second opinion is perhaps the
> most telling symptom of change fatigue because it suggests an ex-
> haustion of judgment. (pp. 10–11)

Teachers also suffer from change fatigue. They are constantly asked to respond to curriculum policy changes, new testing and accountability procedures, and social problems, such as drugs and teen pregnancy. There is little, or no in-service to help with these changes and thus teachers are asked to do more with less. This is one of the "rocks" that Dalla Costa refers to that contributes to change fatigue, which he calls being "Paralyzed by Paradox." Dalla Costa states that asking people "to do more with less" or "do better with fewer" leaves people confused and disheartened. Costa states, as a result of these phony paradoxes, that "purpose has been lost, vision obfuscated, and credibility compromised" (p. 13).

Another "rock" that Dalla Costa discusses is information overload. He refers to the problem of information pollution. This is a problem that he defines as individuals being overwhelmed by so much data that they lose focus. In our society and in schools, information pollution has made it difficult to acquire knowledge and wisdom. Another problem that Dalla Costa identifies is that when people *feel* that they are informed they can sometimes then believe that they are experts. This, then, prevents deeper forms of learning. Some educators argue that technology, including the computer and the Internet, should be the main focus of schooling. Yet these tools, however useful, rarely let us see into the deeper nature of things.

The rocks that Dalla Costa refers to, as well the problem of chronic fatigue, are usually part of organizations that are *mechanistic* in nature (Secretan 1996). Again, many schools fall into this category. The mechanical organization is characterized by "performance measures, strategic planning models, organization charts" (Secretan 1995, p. 33). In schools, we have outcomes, rubrics, and performance indicators. In the mechanistic organization or school there is little opportunity for "innovation, creativity, fun or adventure" and if they are used they tend to be labeled "touchy-feely thinking." Secretan asserts that the result is an organization that is heavily weighted to the masculine and, thus, leads to the inevitable repression of feminine energy. The successful mechanistic school is one where students score highly on standardized test scores but have little interest in how the school is helping to develop whole human beings. Teachers usually suffer from change fatigue in the mechanistic school, while students tend to find the school a cold and non-invitational place.

The second type of organization described by Secretan is the *chaotic* organization. This is based on the notion of chaos theory that suggests that underlying disorder is order and structure. Thus smoke rising from a chimney looks as though it is spiraling in a chaotic manner. Yet each movement can be explained through some mathematical formulae that can also explain other activity such as the swirling of sand grains, the collision of subatomic particles in an electrical resistor, and also the behavior of people in organizations. (Secretan 1996, p. 34). The chaotic organization is characterized by "high energy, enthusiasm, innovation, risk-taking, survival, growth, focused strategy, commitment to the customer, hands-on practices, lack of complexity" (Secretan 1995, p. 35). Sometimes, the chaotic organization is hybrid of the mechanistic organization and the chaotic. Within it, there still may goal-dominated and linear behavior that is linked with the spontaneity of the chaotic organization. Secretan suggests that power and control are the defining characteristics of the mechanical organization, while fun and spontaneity are the characteristics of chaotic organizations. Secretan gives the example of Microsoft as a chaotic organization.

A chaotic school would be characterized by lots of innovation and the teachers and students enjoying what they were doing. Spontaneity and fun would also be hallmarks of the chaotic school. However, there is also an underlying order that insures that learning and growth is occurring.

Secretan defines the soulful organization, calling it the *sanctuary*. For Secretan, the sanctuary is "not a collection of parts but an integrated system of souls—not so much a place but a state of mind in which they may flourish" (Secretan, p. 38). In the sanctuary, people's feelings are acknowledged, as well as their thoughts. Human solutions are not diminished by technological solutions. The soulful school, then, feels like the sanctuary. Both teachers and students look forward to being at school, as they feel that their souls are nourished by the environment they find there. This environment is one of respect, caring, and even reverence. People in the soulful school feel validated as human beings and can speak authentically from their hearts. Love predominates rather than fear. When people speak, they feel that they are heard, often at a heart-centered level. Most of all, there is a deep sense of community. In fact, in the sanctuary, people don't just communicate or exchange ideas: they experience communion with one another. Communion is where soul touches soul.

The sanctuary, like the chaotic organization, also includes spontaneity and fun. It nurtures creativity. The student and the teacher feel comfortable taking risks in their learning. Learning is at the heart of the soulful school. In the mechanical school, the focus is on testing and grades, often at the expense of learning (Cohn 1995). The learning in the soulful school, however, is holistic learning that integrates body mind, emotions, and spirit.

There are no recipes for developing a sanctuary, or a soulful school. However, we can begin to create conditions that allow for the development of soul. Some of the things that a school staff can do include:

1. *Recognize the importance of the nonverbal.* Diana Hughes who is head of the teacher education program of the Ruldolf Steiner Centre in Toronto states that holistic education occurs in that invisible space between teacher and student. It could be argued too that soulful learning also occurs in that place. What does this mean in practice? When we focus on the nonverbal, or that silent space, we become aware of how we carry ourselves, how we engage others through eye contact, and the tone of our voice. We realize that the quality of our being and presence has as much impact on student development as anything that we say. When we become aware of the nonverbal, then a balance can develop between talk and silence. At all levels, education has focused on the head and verbal exchange. We have forgotten about the rest of our bodies and how we can communicate in silence. A warm smile directed to a child can send a message of support and love.

2. *Pay attention to the aesthetic environment of the school and classroom.* We can help transform schools into sanctuaries by making the physical environment more beautiful. For example, plants can become part of the school decor in the halls and in the classrooms. Walls can be painted in soft, warm colors. Artwork, both student artwork and professional artwork, can be placed on the walls. However, there needs to be a balance between artwork that is put on the walls and the surrounding space. Sometimes school classrooms are completely covered so that we cannot really notice what is there. So don't overdo it and leave plenty of space around the art that is put up. In the Waldorf classrooms for the younger children, there are sometimes pictures of the Madonna and child, as they feel the warmth of this picture can have a healing effect on the children. As much as possible, we can soften the school environment.

Some classrooms have couches where students can sit and read.

3. *Tell stories about the school.* Every school has a story or, more accurately, a set of stories. Teachers and students can collect these stories and put them together in a booklet or tell them on special school occasions. If stories are shared over time teachers and students can begin to see the continuity and uniqueness of their school. The process of collecting stories can be helpful as students interview former students or members of the surrounding community. Sketches (both written and visual) can be constructed of former teachers and students. The set of stories eventually can create a mythology for the school. This mythology is a shared sense of meaning and values for the school. By telling stories about the school recurring themes will emerge that can form the heart of the school's mythology. For example, do the stories tend to focus on academic achievement, sports, or community service, or some combination of the three? Private schools often engage in this practice of telling stories and creating a shared sense of meaning, but I see no reason that this cannot also happen in the public school, which also has its own unique history.

4. *Have celebrations and rituals.* This suggestion is closely related to the last one. Rituals help give people a sense of connection to their communities. The most common ritual and celebration in schools is graduation. While this is one time when there is a chance to share stories of the school, there is no reason to limit rituals and celebrations to this one event. Celebrations could be conducted to mark changes in the seasons. These celebrations could include playing music, reading poetry, and telling stories. Rituals can be part of the daily life of the school. In one school, discussed later in this chapter, the students of the entire school meet every morning to sing and perhaps listen to an elder from the community. This meeting every morning helps form a deep sense of community in the school.

5. *Truth and Authenticity.* Secretan argues that telling the truth is an important aspect of cultivating soul in the workplace. When we live in an atmosphere where people are not telling the truth, integrity and community break down. In the 1960s the term "credibility gap" appeared, particularly around the Vietnam War, as government officials' credibil-

ity began to be questioned. As much as possible, leaders should attempt to speak and live according to what they see as truth. We should recognize that we are imperfect human beings but also that our integrity comes from our ability to live authentic lives. We have certain clichés about this process and one of the most frequently cited is that "he or she walks the talk." One of the behaviors that helps build authenticity is promise keeping. When we keep our promises, others can learn to depend on our word. Sometimes in schools, gaps can develop between what we espouse and what we do. For example, a principal might talk about the importance of collegial decision making and then make all the important decisions on his or her own. When a gap develops between what a principal says and does, cynicism develops. Trust is almost nonexistent. On the other hand, when we work with someone who we feel is trustworthy and authentic we can feel empowered. Energy seems to arise in place of trust while it dissipates in an atmosphere of nontrust. This energy can empower others to take risks and be creative.

6. *Nourishing Voice.* A soulful school is a place where people can speak without fear. I would like to cite David Whyte (1994):

> Inhabiting the full body, the long body, as many North American Native traditions say, with the voice, may be one of the great soul challenges of adult life. If the voice originates and ends its journey in the bodies of the speaker and listener, it is also true that many parts of our bodies are struck deaf or dumb from an early age. We walk through the door into organization every morning looking like full-grown adults but many parts of us are still playing emotional catch-up. (p. 127)

Whyte suggests that one of the ways we can reclaim our voice is to learn to say no. By saying no we gradually learn to say yes to what we ultimately value and feel is important to our soul. Of course, of the leaders in our schools must be comfortable cultivating an environment where voice can be heard. The principal needs to be aware, of course, his or her voice. Each person needs to ask himself or herself where I am speaking from? Am I speaking mostly from my head or from the deeper part of myself?

SOULFUL SCHOOLS

In this section we will look at some schools that have put into practice some of the principles outlined above.

Fratney School

This school is an inner-city school, in Milwaukee, Wisconsin, that was formed in 1988 by a group of parents who wanted a two-way bilingual school (English/Spanish). The goal of the school is to enable the student to speak and write in both languages by grade 5. Students begin work in their mother tongue and then gradually include the other language. The school was formed on certain principles: bilingual, whole language, multicultural, and gender equal. Learning focuses around major themes such as

> Our Roots in the School and Community
> The New Native American Experience
> The African American Experience
> The Hispanic Experience
> The Asian American/Pacific American Experience
> We Are a Multicultural nation. (Wood, p. 21)

George Wood, who included this school in his book *Schools That Work* (1992), suggests that this school is successful, in part, because of the focus on community and cooperation in the class-room. Teachers involve students in setting classroom rules. Also, cooperation is the predominant mode rather than competition. Each classroom develops a conflict-resolution structure so that problems can be "resolved within the spirit of maintaining the classroom community" (p. 23).

The school is run by a team that consists of parent representatives, representatives from the staff, and the principal. This team basically makes all the major decisions about what happens at Fratney. One parent sums up why she sent her daughter to Fratney:

> *Why Fratney?*
> When time grew near for [our daughter] to begin her school year we were concerned. She was on the waiting list for several schools, but not high enough. Then we heard about Fratney. A group of parents, frustrated with even some of the best schools in the system, and some "young Turk" teachers, some of the most talented and principled educators in the city, were coming together to form a school where

decisions would be made on site. Those involved consciously decided to have an anti-racist, non-sexist curriculum. The children would learn that we are all together on this planet and that what we and our teachers do every day affects every person and place. Our responsibility to each other is to care and nurture and provide a successful experience for all our students. (Wood, p. 25)

Hope Nursery School

This is a new school that opened in Annapolis, Maryland, in 1990. It is founded on the principles of the Japanese educator, Tsunesaburo Makiguchi (1989). Makiguchi believed education should foster values in three different areas: "1) economic value or private gain; 2) moral value or public gain, and 3) aesthetic value relating to the senses" (Bliss, p. 53). Bliss then describes how these values are explored in a unit on trees:

> We examine economic or personal value, such as, "How can fallen leaves benefit us?"; moral or social value, as how our planting a tiny tree benefits the community; and aesthetic value, as how the beauty of the fall foliage inspires us in aesthetics and ecology. As we walk through the woods, we sometimes gather "treasures" such as leaves or seed travelers, and at other times we gather trash. When our recycling barrel is full, we take a class trip to the recycling center. We also visited a neighbor who sheltered injured birds for the state department of wildlife, watched and fed the birds, and became acquainted with a woman who acts on her values in caring for wildlife. (p. 53)

Although the school is based on Makiguchi's principles, it also incorporates principles from other educators such as Montessori. The school uses a thematic approach to curriculum, where disciplines are integrated around major themes. These themes are usually connected to real life experience. For example, in studying homes and shelters, the students build shelters from sand or snow and also look for animal shelters in the woods. Bliss (1992) notes:

> We practice using real hammers and saws and hand drills for manual competence; measure our shelters and map them together; discuss forms of energy used in our homes; identify forms of shelters used in different environments by primitive peoples from Townley's (1978) art curriculum entitled *Another Look;* sort puzzle pieces or various architectural styles that require careful discrimination of detail; sing

the Afro-American song "Old House"; and discuss personal, social, and aesthetic values as we create a neighborhood of paper houses. (p. 54)

The Hope School also attempts to provide what might be called a "soulful" physical environment for students to work and play in. The room is carpeted and is meant to have the feel of home rather than an institution. For example, there is a couch where both adults and children can sit as stories are read. Classical music is played while the children work and there is often an artist-in-residence whose works are displayed.

Finally every attempt is made to link the school to the family and surrounding community. The school involves parents in the life of the school and encourages the parents to reflect on their own approaches to child-rearing and learning.

The Environmental Middle School

This is an alternative school that began in 1995, within the framework of the Portland public school system. The school consists of 135 adolescents, seven teachers, and many parents and volunteers. There are five mixed-age classes from grades 6, 7, and 8. The school is based partly on the thinking of Thomas Moore. Taking inspiration from his concepts, some of the activities are designed to help nourish the student's soul. These include: "the morning meeting; preparation of the community meal; contact with nature; and participation in community service" (Williams et al., p. 19).

The daily morning meeting is seen as a ritual that involves the entire school community. One of the teachers, John Richter, plays a guitar and teaches everyone to sing. The songs focus on peace and care of the earth and people involved in the school feel that to have students sing together with staff and parents helps create a deep bond within the school community.

The morning meetings also involve storytelling, usually by elders from the community. On other occasions, teachers can present on topics of interest to the whole community. For example, one day a teacher made a presentation on bats and used slides to show "bat habitats, their features, their classifications, what they ate, what they liked, where they lived in Oregon, and which were endangered species" (Williams et al., p. 19). The next day, John Richter presented a song he had written about bats. These meetings were then followed by an activity where students made bat houses for distribution to people in the community.

Another important feature of the school is community service. Students are encouraged to do a variety of activities in the community. Some of the activities have included:

> planting trees at the local arboretum; distributing brochures in the neighborhood to save the elms from Dutch Elm disease; pulling ivy from trees at one of the creeks in the city; building raised garden beds for the elderly and creating handicapped-accessible community gardens; feeding the hungry at a local homeless shelter; making and distributing birdhouses to the elderly; and naturescaping and planting trees for ecological restoration in the city's watersheds. (Williams et al., p. 21)

Community service activities such as those described above also can nourish soul as they can foster deeper connections to others.

Thomas Moore also claims that sharing meals and good conversation is nourishing for the body and the soul. So, once a month, one of the classes will prepare a meal for the entire school community.

Finally, the students participate in ecological projects that are not an add-on to the curriculum but are integrated into the curriculum's core. For example, one term the entire curriculum was organized around the theme of rivers. The students picked a river in the United States and then studied the river from a variety of perspectives: historical, geographical, and environmental. The students also read "historical novels; created art projects; sang songs on rivers; performed experiments and studied about water properties; learned about water conservation techniques in their own homes and monitored streams as they participated in streamwalks" (p. 22).

Soule School

Yes, there actually is a school explicitly based on the concept of soul. It is an alternative school that exists within the Freeport, Maine public school system. The school has a creed that was developed by students, teachers, and parents in 1975.

> We believe that children should be encouraged to be self-directing, to make decisions and accept the consequences.
>
> We believe that children need time to follow their interests, to experience success and failure—in other words, to give the child practice in some of the behaviors that make responsible adults.

We believe that children should have the freedom to pursue their personal interests and goals and to develop new ones.

We believe that children should be encouraged to think for themselves and to take responsibility for their actions.

We believe that children should have the total community as their learning environment and should be taken to every possible place of interest.

We believe that children should practice self-government and should come to feel important as part of the school community by participation in decisions that affect the school.

We believe that children should be allowed to work and play with children of other ages in a family-like atmosphere.

We believe that children should evaluate their own progress, have regular input into their curriculum, and take some responsibility for the planning and carrying-through of related learning activities.

We believe that children should feel good about themselves, and should meet regularly for the opportunity to discuss their feelings and concerns.

We believe that children should have fun in school.

We believe that children should have personal freedom, but not at the expense of the freedom of others.

We believe that teachers should identify individual needs and make provisions for work at different levels of difficulty and for different styles of learning.

We believe that teachers should take children's ideas into consideration when planning learning activities.

We believe that teachers should provide an environment of mutual trust and understanding—an environment that is warm, loving, relaxed, and non-competitive.

We believe that, where appropriate, teachers should share decision-making with parents and students.

We believe that teachers should recognize that the learning process is usually as important as its content.

We believe that teachers should report students' progress by stating what they have accomplished.

We believe that teachers should be encouraged to expand the basic curriculum by bringing their own interests into the classroom.

We believe that teachers should enjoy their work and share their enthusiasm with the students and each other.

We believe that teachers should be available and unshockable so that children will not have to live with unnecessary guilt for their human behavior.

We believe that teachers should foster a close association with parents based on honest communication.

We believe that teachers should have personal freedom, but not at the expense of the freedom of others.

We believe that parents should play an active role in the education of their children and in the Soule School program.

Recently, a former teacher and student have examined this creed in relation to the work of Thomas Moore (1992). Peter Corcoran and Eric Horne (1996) state that "Soule School was a place that appreciated the existence of soul as a matter of depth, value, relatedness, heart, personal substance, genuineness, attachment, love and community as described by Moore" (p. 25). It also recognized the importance of world soul as the school has attempted to connect the students to the surrounding communities both human and natural. Students meet together in a "Big Meeting" and small groups to discuss important issues. According to Corcoran and Horne, these meetings help develop a sense of community through listening. Horne describes the "Big Meeting" as a place where students could state their views about anything from "teacher smoking to snowball fights." Corcoran also comments on the importance of listening to students which was an essential element in the school.

> As teachers, it behooves us to listen as well as to lecture. Departing from abstract discussion at times to move to issues of the students' "lived lives" brings depth and power to classroom life. (p. 26)

An important part of school life is connecting the student to nature, which Moore believes is healing (p. 12). The natural environment of Maine provides an excellent setting for this connection.

Teachers in the school also accept the shadow side of the student which Moore says is an integral part of soul. This is reflected in one of the belief statements of the school: "We believe that teachers should be available and unshockable so that children will not have to live with unnecessary guilt for their human behavior" (p. 25).

Peter, who taught at Soule School, felt that his work had a strong impact on his other work after he left the school. For example, he continued using group meetings to deal with student issues and he also used ritual, which was part of the Soule School. He writes, "After inviting students to lead opening activities for class, yoga, tai chi, and meditation became fairly regular opening rituals.

Indeed the importance of ritual has become clear to me in caring for the soul" (p. 26). Corcoran and Horne describe the Soule School as a place where students and teachers wanted to be.

> We never knew a child who didn't want to come to school. Even the most doubting parents were persuaded by this passionate love of school. Children cried at vacations and, at the end of Soule School, were known to cry for days. Teachers, too, loved the place passionately and almost never did one leave other than to go to graduate school. (p. 25)

It is apparent that this school created Secretan's sanctuary.

If people who work in schools can bring an awareness of soul into the workplace I believe that the type of atmosphere described by Corcoran and Horne could arise in other schools. Bringing soul into the school will not be done through plans or implementation models but through the awareness and sensitivity of each staff member. Through this awareness we can bring a new vitality to schools that is so often missing. In the film *Mr. Holland's Opus,* the new music teacher comments that he knew that the kids didn't like high school but as a new teacher he learned that teachers hated school as well. Bringing soul into the school can make schools places where both students and teachers want to be.

FINAL THOUGHTS

Waldorf schools are also good examples of soul schools. In chapter 5 I discussed briefly Steiner's theory of development and how one teacher approached the visual arts in his classroom. Waldorf teachers openly acknowledge and communicate about the soul life of the children. The physical environment, the aesthetic surroundings, the curriculum, the teacher's presence are all viewed in the context of how they can nurture the inner life of the child. One of the key aspects of Waldorf education is that the children's main lesson teacher works with the same group of children from grades 1 to 8 so that he or she can develop a strong connection to the students and the classroom can take on an almost family-like atmosphere. The curriculum itself is rich in stories and images that also nourish soul. One example of how the teacher can consciously work with the soul life of the child is that in the evening the teacher sometimes will try to visualize the child and what will help in the development of the inner life of that child.

8

The Soulful Teacher

The teacher sets the tone and the atmosphere of the classroom. If the student's soul is to be nurtured and developed, it follows then that the process must begin with the teacher's soul. If the teacher's soul is contracted and impoverished, then there is little chance that the student's soul will be adequately cared for. Teachers who cannot bring their authentic presence to the classroom each day, who cannot attune themselves empathetically to their students are ill-equipped to give of themselves or respond appropriately to students' needs.

In this chapter, I discuss how we can nurture the teacher's soul in ways that will make teaching richer and more fulfilling. Nurturing soul requires a radically different approach to professional development. Generally, professional development has focused on: teaching strategies, classroom management skills, the implementation of new curriculum and student assessment policies. Of course, many of these activities are important but ultimately they occur within the framework of soul. To ignore soul is to overlook an essential element in learning and development.

CONTEMPLATION

As discussed in several sections of this book, contemplation is essential to the soul and to bring the lessons of the soul into the conscious mind where they can enter into our daily life. A linear, rationalistic approach to thinking and living tends to predominate in our culture and, thus, opportunities for the soul's growth are limited.

Linear approaches to thinking and professional development often focus on mechanistic theories. Teachers learn to use a "model" in the specified correct way as they learn a set of steps or strategies that go with the model. This technical approach has been

criticized by Schon (1983), who argued for the importance of reflection. Schon draws on the work of Polyani (1962) who states that
the "the aim of a skillful performance is achieved by the observance
of a set of rules which are not known as such to the person following
them" (p. 49). Reflection, then, is based on what Polyani has called
"tacit knowing," or intuition, that guides moment-to-moment actions. Schon calls this "reflection-in-action." Reflection-in-action
refers to skillful performance that tends to have the following
qualities:

> There are actions, recognitions, and judgments which we know how
> to carry out spontaneously; we do not have to think about them prior
> to or during their performance.
>
> We are often unaware of having learned to do these things; we
> simply find ourselves doing them.
>
> In some cases, we were once aware of the understandings which
> were subsequently internalized in our feeling for the stuff of action.
> In other cases, we may never have been aware of them. In both cases,
> however, we are usually unable to describe the knowing which our
> action reveals. (p. 54)

Schon cites, as an example, the jazz musician as someone who
uses reflection-in-action to improvise and play music. There is a
constant shifting of consciousness and activity, and reflection
guides this process. In education, Schon (1983) quotes Tolstoy to
give an example of reflection in an educational setting.

> Every individual must, in order to acquire the art of reading in the
> shortest possible time, be taught quite apart from any other, and
> therefore there must be a separate method for each. That which
> forms an insuperable difficulty to one does not in the least keep back
> another and vice versa. One pupil has a good memory, and it is easier
> for him to memorize the syllables than to comprehend the vowelless-
> ness of the consonants; another reflects calmly and will comprehend
> a most rational sound method; another has a fine instinct, and he
> grasps the law of word combinations by reading whole words at a
> time.
>
> The best teacher will be he who has at his tongue's end the
> explanation of what it is that is bothering the pupil. These explana-
> tions give the teacher the knowledge of the greatest possible number
> of methods, the ability of inventing new methods and, above all, not
> a blind adherence to one method but the conviction that all meth-
> ods are one-sided, and that the best method would be one which

would answer best to all the possible difficulties incurred by a pupil, that is, not a method but an art and talent.

> Every teacher must. . . . by regarding every imperfection in the pupil's comprehension, not as a defect of the pupil, but as a defect of his own instruction, endeavor to develop in himself the ability of discovering new methods. (pp. 65–66)

So Schon and many other educators have encouraged the development of what is called "reflective practice." Like Tolstoy, effective teachers reflect on their teaching, both during and after practice.

Reflective practice is important in bringing the intuitive into consciousness where it can be acted upon. But it is not to be confused with contemplation. Nor is it a replacement for contemplation, because it is in contemplation where new horizons for the soul are opened, new lessons learned. In contemplation, boundaries disappear as we attempt to become the object that we contemplate. As we contemplate a beautiful piece of art or music, at some point we don't feel separate from the music or art. We feel it becomes part of our being, or soul.

One way of developing our contemplative capacities is through meditation. Over the past ten years I have introduced teachers to meditative practice in two courses that I teach at the Ontario Institute for Studies in Education/University of Toronto (OISE/UT). OISE/UT provides graduate programs in education, as well as field services to teachers and schools. I participate in both of these activities but it is in my teaching where I have introduced meditation to graduate students in education.

I teach two courses: Holistic Education and The Teacher as Contemplative Practitioner. In both courses, I require students to meditate every day, for about six weeks. I ask students to do the meditation because I believe that teaching is best done when we work from our souls rather than from our egos. If teaching is ego-based, it often becomes an act of control and thus, as teachers, we often end up in little battles with our students. However, if we can teach from our souls and spirits, then we begin to see ourselves in the students and them in us. Teaching then becomes a different act where learning and exploration can occur in an atmosphere of freedom, love, and respect.

The students in my classes are experienced teachers, between thirty and fifty-five years old. They are mostly female (e.g., seventy-five percent). Most come from Ontario but OISE/UT draws a large number of international students. I have had students from Brazil,

China, Indonesia, Israel, Italy, Jamaica, Japan, Kenya, Malta, Nigeria, Poland, and Russia.

The large majority of these students have never meditated before. Many are skeptical in the beginning. I have made meditation a requirement of these courses since 1988 and, up to the time of this writing, I have introduced approximately 850 students to meditation practice. Only two students have asked not to do the meditation. Their reasons were varied. One had been sexually assaulted a year before and did not feel comfortable with the practice. The other was a fundamentalist Christian. My courses are electives and the enrollment is always filled, with a waiting list of others wanting to get in. I believe that many students now take the course *because* of the meditation requirement.

Although, I myself have been doing insight (vipassana) meditation for over twenty years, I introduce the students to four or five basic approaches to meditation. These usually include meditation on the breath, mantra, visualization, movement, and lovingkindness. Whatever form students choose, I emphasize that in meditation we let go of the calculating mind and open ourselves to the listening mind that tends to be characterized by a *relaxed alertness*. Once the students have settled on a method for the duration of the course, I encourage them to work up to about thirty minutes a day of meditation practice. I keep in touch with each student through journals they keep on their practice. In the journals, I ask students to focus on the process of meditation (e.g., how they are focusing, how their body feels, etc.) and not the content of any thoughts that arise.

I should also mention that I start each of my classes with a form of lovingkindness meditation (e.g., may all beings be well, happy, and peaceful). Finally, I also introduce students to the practice of mindfulness in daily life so that they can live more in moment-to-moment awareness. I will describe both of these practices in this chapter.

Most students experience frustration in the first week or two. They want to know whether they are doing meditation in the "right" way and often are very judgmental about their practice. One student's statement is typical:

> *In the beginning, I was never sure if I was "doing it right." I became annoyed if a session did not go well. Now, I am much more relaxed about it. I realize that every session will not go "well" and that there is no prescribed experience.*
> (Cited in Miller 1995, p.19)

Another student commented:

In the beginning it was extremely difficult for me to sit. . . . At least this is how
I initially perceived the exercise to be. I had to fight with myself not to get up
and give up. Five minutes seemed like an eternity and it was quite painful.
But only a few days later I noticed that I felt a little more at peace with myself
as a result of this brief moment I had spent meditating. Once I discovered this
feeling I wanted to explore it more.

For the large majority of students the intense frustration
disappears after a week or two. Students begin to let go of immediate expectations. One student put it this way: "There were a few
frustrating days at this point when I felt like giving up. I wasn't
getting anywhere. But then I decided there was nowhere to get to,
no place I had to be!"

Many of the students mention the *letting go* as an important
shift in their meditation. One teacher stated: "As those clouds of
thoughts passed by me in my mind I was amazed at how adept I
became at not letting them stay. No matter how strong the image I
found that I had the strength to 'let go.'" Another teacher related
this letting go to her work: "However, focusing and re-focusing on
the natural rhythm of breathing or walking helped me to 'let go'
and feel the stress lighten and/or disappear. This made me a more
relaxed teacher and I was able to move on with my day with a
renewed sense of energy."

The ego tries to control events while the soul attunes itself to
different rhythms in life. One student made this shift from ego to
soul while listening to music:

I didn't intend to meditate at the symphony but I learned something in the
course of the evening. The second selection was a Bach Concerto for Two
Violins. It started with a vigorous "Vivace" and then switched to a "Largo," I
noticed that my breathing altered substantially from one section to the other
and found myself breathing slowly during the Largo. The meditation seemed
to flow easily. I wasn't following the music as much as the rhythm. That's
when I realized that meditation, for me anyway, should not be a matter of
control, but rather rhythm. (Cited in Miller 1994, p. 126)

Most students report that meditation has given them a renewed sense of energy and general sense of well being. One student
reported: "After meditation I often felt re-energized. It seemed to
take the tiredness of the day away, if I didn't do it too late at night."
Another teacher linked this renewed energy to an increased ability
to focus on her work: "I am meeting deadlines, as I did before, but
without the feeling of panic that I might not get it all done. I seem

to have more energy and awakened ability to focus and concentrate on the job at hand."

Many students report a new awareness of their bodies. One student mentioned: "The first major effect of meditating that I was aware of was on my physical self. I had not realized how much tension I carried in my neck and shoulders." Another student reported:

> It [meditation] has taught me quite a bit about my body. It is interesting that our body does so much for us throughout our lives and yet we really don't notice it. During meditation, I could feel it. The movements inside, the twitches of the muscles, etc. I found it interesting to read through my journal and find that my body was actually indicating the onset of my illness. Now that I am able to read this message it will be interesting to see how I can better use the information to attend to my body's needs.

Students learn not only to listen to the body but listen in all areas of their life. They report how more deeply they listen to other people and to all the sounds around them. One student wrote:

> I have been a radio-aholic, with the CBC on at all times. However, I leave it off during meditation, and have become even more aware of the bird calls that are all around. I have taken to opening the window before I begin so that I won't miss them! The sound of the wind through the leaves is also a tremendously calming sound. The sounds of nature around me are very important and I have become aware of them and the need to let them in.

Students also comment on how meditation gives them permission to be alone and nurture their own souls. Many of my students are women in midlife with families and teaching responsibilities. They are constantly "on the go."

> As a relaxing strategy it [meditation] has offered a time to get to know me better and to understand me and why I do the things that I do and that most importantly that I am OK. I am an important person for me to get to know and to spend time with. It is a time that I enjoy and have come to need. . . . A time to be with me with no one making demands or needing assistance. I have come to need these minutes to myself. (Cited in Miller 1994, p. 127)

Joan Borysenko (1995) has written "Soul, the basic substance of the universe, yearns for connection" (p. 47). Many of my students have moments where the barriers drop away and they experience a deep interconnectedness with life. One student wrote:

126

*I concentrated on my breathing patterns and I slipped into a familiar stance.
Little entered my mind, I was simply enjoying the sensations of peace and
tranquillity. When I awoke, I left the apartment and walked home. I noticed
that I was humming and strolling with a light step.*

*Children on their bicycles and little puppies in my path were making me
smile. In this remote corner of the world, all was calm. I realized after awhile
that I was mirroring the image of my surroundings and in a small way, it felt
wonderful to be part of the serenity of life.*

*In essence I felt that I have participated in education of introspection, as
well as, the experience of interconnectedness with other people, with the surrounding nature, and with the infinite universe.* (Cited in Miller 1994, pp.
129–30)

Another student put his experience of dropping boundaries this
way.

*The session began with many thoughts and physical sensations which quickly
settled down, and although they didn't totally disappear, were not much in my
awareness afterward. It was a very quiet and uneventful meditation with the
mantra barely present. In fact there was not much present at all except the
awareness of myself just being there. This continued until towards the end of
the session when I began to have certain feelings or knowledge; it's hard to
explain how the two combine into one. It's like you know something with every
cell of your body, to the point that you actually feel it everywhere. . . . I was
keenly aware that I was part of all that was around me. There was no
distinction between my inner self, my body, and my surroundings. This awareness extended out so that I felt a part of all that there is. As I read what I'm
writing, the words sound quite grandiose, whereas the experience was very
simple. However, it was also profound, peaceful and fulfilling at all levels:
physical, intellectual, and spiritual.* (Cited in Miller 1994, p. 130)

Certainly these experiences are contemplative ones. Some
people, of course, are fearful of dropping boundaries. When our
egos are predominant then we want to keep ourselves separate.

In sum, one of the main reasons for introducing meditation
to teachers is that it is a highly nourishing experience for the soul.
Much if not almost all of our day is spent in ego-planning and
calculating. Very little of this activity is conducive to soul, so that
thirty minutes of meditation is a very small amount of time compared to the time that is ego-driven.

Below are some of the meditations that I introduce to teachers. They are outlined here as well for the reader who would like to
begin his or her own practice. They are described in somewhat
more detail in *The Contemplative Practitioner.*

Breath Meditation

One of the simplest, most natural meditations is on the breath. It is one of the most organic meditations since it focuses on a natural body rhythm. The person simply focuses the awareness on breath as it comes in through the nostrils down the esophagus and into the lungs. The awareness then follows the breath during exhalation, as the abdomen contracts and the air is released through the nostrils. To keep focused, the individual may want to silently repeat "in" on the in breath and "out" on the outbreath.

Of course, thoughts will enter during this process but we can simply note the thought and let it go. We can see thoughts just as thoughts and we don't have to give them more power than they are due. Avoid any attempt to control the breathing; instead just follow the rhythm of the breathing. Notice whether it is fast or slow, deep or shallow. Most importantly, do not judge the process. All day, we are evaluating what is happening to us and there is tendency to carry this over to meditation. Don't. Just accept what is happening in the moment.

A variation on this meditation is to count the breaths. Some people like the structure that counting provides and feel that it helps provide more focus. We can count the breath as we exhale. In Zen, the recommended practice is counting up to ten while LeShan (1974) recommends counting to just four. It is not unusual to go over the number limit (e.g., 10 or 4). If you do, just note this nonjudgmentally and return to counting one.

Breathing is also the starting point for insight, or vipassana meditation. However, it is just a starting point or anchor. Although the meditator starts with the breath, he or she gradually expands awareness to other factors such as body sensations, feelings, sounds in the environment, and thoughts. The person focuses on what is predominant in the moment. Thus, if there is a loud noise the attention shifts to that sound. When the sound disappears, then it is back to the breath. Gradually, the person develops moment-to-moment awareness. This is a complex meditation and should be learned with an instructor, ideally in a retreat setting. One of the best books on this form of meditation is *The Experience of Insight* by Joseph Goldstein (1976). This book includes instructions and talks given over a thirty-day meditation retreat.

Mantra: Meditation on Sound

Mantra, or meditation on sound, is also a form of meditation that many individuals find effective. In this practice a word, a sound or phrase is used as the focus of attention. The intent of the practice is to attune yourself to the mantra and its rhythm. If the ego is too much in play you will try to control the rhythm rather than finding the rhythm. Carrington (1977) makes the point:

> That is all there is to meditating—just sitting peacefully, hearing the mantra in your mind, allowing it to change any way it wants—to get louder or softer—to disappear or return—to stretch out or speed up. . . . Meditation is like drifting in a boat without oars—you are not going anywhere. (p. 80)

Some mantras are simply sounds (e.g., Ah-nam) while others have religious or spiritual significance. The Catholic rosary can be viewed as a mantra as well as the Jesus prayer: "Jesus, have mercy on me."

In the first case the sound acts as the center of awareness and the sound itself may have effects on the soul. In the second instance, the phrase allows the soul to become united with what is being repeated. For example, at a young age Gandhi learned the mantra "Ram," which is one name of God in Hinduism. By repeating this mantra throughout his life, Gandhi felt he become closer to the divine. It is said that he died with the word "Ram" on his lips.

Visualization

While mantra uses sound as a point of focus, visualization or guided imagery uses an image or set of images. Usually, there is a scripted sequence of images and events that tend to evoke images within the person. Visualization was discussed extensively in chapter 4 so I will not say much here about the process. Working with teachers, visualizations can focus on issues related to their aspirations.

> Relax. . . . Close your eyes. . . . You are in a meadow. . . . The sky is blue and you see a hill in the distance. . . . What does the hill look like as you approach it? . . . Is the hill large or small? . . . . Is it rough and hard to climb or is its surface smooth and easy to scale? . . . You see a path going up the hill and you follow it. . . . Is the path wide or narrow? . . . What is the ground like around you as you begin to walk up the path? . . . Is there grass or are there lots of rocks. . . . As you walk up this hill notice the view. . . . Stop and look around. . . . How far can you see? . . . Now begin to resume your walk. . . . Smell the fresh air as you walk up the path. . . . You feel invigorated and refreshed as you walk up the hill. . . .

You begin to approach the top of the hill and there you see a temple. . . . As you approach the temple what does it look like? . . . Notice the form of the building as you approach it. . . . As you approach the temple you feel peaceful and calm. . . . You walk to the door of the temple and take your shoes off. . . . There is an opening at the top of the temple roof and sunlight is steaming through. . . . You walk to the light and stand under it and feel its radiance and warmth. . . . Let it permeate and rejuvenate your whole being. . . . You are now ready to go the inner sanctuary. . . . There is a symbol or an image in the center of the room. . . . This symbol represents to you an educational ideal. . . . Reflect on this symbol and its meaning for you. . . . [two or three minute pause] Leave the temple and walk slowly down the hill. . . . Take the energy you have received from this journey and use it as you return to your daily life. (Miller 1993, p. 78–9)

A collection of guided imagery exercises for adults can be found in Ferrucci's book: *What We May Be*. Most of the exercises in Ferucci's book come from nature. Many guided imagery exercises include images from nature. Some of these images and their possible meanings include:

Water: receptivity, passivity, calm
Ascent: growth, inward journey
Cross: tree of life, spiritual connectedness
Hill or Mountain: aims or ambitions
Light: creativity, unity, spiritual source
Sun: life force, healing spiritual wholeness

(Samuels and Samuels, p. 97)

One of my colleagues at OISE/UT, David Hunt (1987, 1992), has explored the concept of guided imagery as a vehicle to facilitate the teacher's development. He has used it extensively with students in his classes in a variety of ways. He sees imagery, for example, as a way of renewing personal energy.

Visualization can also be used as a way to connect with students. In Waldorf schools it is the practice that the teacher in the evening will visualize one or two students in his or her class. This way, the teacher senses the inner needs of the student. Through this process, the souls of the teacher and student can connect with each other.

Movement

In this form, we focus the awareness on physical movement. One of the simplest exercises here is to be aware of walking. Walking meditation, then, involves being aware of the lifting and movement of the feet. We are conscious of the lifting of the foot, its movement, and its placement.

There are many other forms of movement meditation. A few of these include yoga, tai ch'i, and aikido. As we focus on the movement of the body, we can become more conscious of how the energy flows through it. It is a Prana yoga exercise to combine breathing meditation with walking. This practice involves counting the breaths with each footstep. Breath in for four steps and out for eight steps. Breath-holding while walking is an advanced practice. While watching our moving bodies, we can note where there is tension or resistance in the body. As we shift our awareness to these places, then, we can release the tension and let the energy flow more easily through the body.

Loving-kindness

This meditation is one that I use to begin my classes. It focuses on the development of compassion for all beings. It begins by sensing a basic warmth in our hearts and then gradually sharing this warmth and compassion with others. For example you can use the following approach:

> May I be well, happy, and peaceful.
> May my family be well, happy, and peaceful.
> May my friends be well, happy, and peaceful.
> May my neighbors be well, happy, and peaceful.
> May my colleagues be well, happy and peaceful,
> May all people that I meet be well, happy, and peaceful.
> May all people who may have injured me by deed, speech, or
>   thought be well, happy, and peaceful.
> May all beings on this planet be well, happy, and peaceful.
> May all beings in this universe be well, happy, and peaceful.

It is also possible to visualize specific people as you do this meditation. Another form of the exercise involves moving outward geographically so that the focus is first on yourself, then beings in the room and building your are in, and then to beings inhabiting the city, district, and hemisphere. Finally, the focus is on the earth and the universe. In the beginning, this may seem artificial, but my experience with my students is that it is a powerful and soulful meditation. In doing this practice we begin to carry a conscious compassion for others deep within our souls. I have said many times to my students and others, that if this meditation was practiced before business and governmental meetings around the globe, the world could become a very different place. Finally, I recommend Sharon Salzberg's *Lovingkindness* as the best introduction to this meditation practice.

Mindfulness

Mindfulness is way to bring soul into our daily lives. When we live mindfully, we are in the here-and-now; we are present and awake. This sounds so simple but for much of our day we live on automatic pilot. We go from one task to another doing the tasks in a routine way or with our consciousness distracted in different directions. For example, we often eat mindlessly as we are watching television or reading the newspaper. We can drive our cars with our minds on everything except the road.

Our students, children, and spouses can usually sense immediately if we are not present. If we are lost in our agenda we can lose touch very quickly with the world around us. We can become like Mr. Duffy in Joyce's *Ulysses* who lives a few feet from his body. If we are like Mr. Duffy a deep alienation can build between ourselves and our students.

I believe that what our students want, more than anything else, is our full authentic presence as a human being. So what can we do to develop this presence? Mother Theresa was asked how she did such great things, and she answered "I simply do small things with great love." So we can do the small things during the day such as preparing a meal or washing the dishes with love and presence. We bring our full attention to the smallest task. Thich Nhat Hahn (1976, 1991) has written several books on mindfulness that include many exercises that we can practice during the day to bring us into the present.

The result of starting with the small things is that we can then bring our attention to the classroom and the result is usually something quite wonderful. I would like to quote again a teacher who brought mindfulness to her classroom.

> *As a teacher, I have become more aware of my students and their feelings in the class. Instead of rushing through the day's events, I take the time to enjoy our*

day's experiences and opportune moments. The students have commented that I seem happier. I do tend to laugh more and I think it is because I am more aware, alert and "present," instead of thinking about what I still need to do. (Miller 1995, p.22)

LIVING CONTEMPLATIVELY

Slowing Down

Slowing down and mindfulness go hand-in-hand. They complement and support each other and both nurture soul. However, slowing down in today's fast-paced world is increasingly difficult. The pressures from all sides is to speed up our lives. We are asked to do more, particularly in our work, as companies are downsized. School systems have also been cut and class sizes increased. As we run from one thing to another, we find that there is so little space. We feel driven. When we live like this, we find little time to connect with our soul, with others, and with the earth.

What can we do to slow down?

1. Drop, or at least shorten, the list. I have learned in reading my students' journals that almost everyone has a list of things to do. Often this list can be quite long and it hangs over us making us feel that we are constantly behind. It can even make us feel inadequate. If we look at the list closely we may find that many of the things we think we need to do are based on consumerism. We simply don't *need* to make that trip to the shopping mall.

2. Create gaps during the day. We can build spaces in our day by sometimes taking a deep breath or simply pausing in what we are doing. We can begin to learn to create space around the things we do through breathing and pausing. We can also intentionally build gaps when are going somewhere. So if you are going to the airport or a meeting give yourself extra time to get there. In contrast, there are some people who are always behind as they are almost always late to meetings and events. Their lives seem a constant struggle to catch up. With the rush to catch up there is little or no opportunity to be in the present moment.

3. Be aware of when you feel the rush taking over. You can often feel your body tense up when you start to go too fast or do many things at once. As soon as you feel the tension arise in the body, consciously make an effort to slow down.

A helpful aid to slowing down is the book *Slowing Down in a Speeded Up World* by Adair Lara (1994). The book includes stories of people slowing down in different ways as well as some suggestions. For example:

> Borrow a small child and follow him or her around for awhile—you'll notice things you haven't seen in years. (p. 9)

> Take your child on a flower walk, sniffing every flower along the way. (p. 63)

Music

Some of the most soulful moments can come through the arts. For many, it can be a piece of music that brings us to a contemplative state and thus lets soul come forth. Music can immediately shift our consciousness from ego to where we feel our souls connected to something larger than ourselves. When I listen to Mozart, this is what I almost always feel even when he expresses anguish in his music. I know of no better expression of soul in music than the following statement by Jacques Lusseyran (1987):

> The world of violins and flutes, of horns and cellos, of fugues, scherzos and gavottes, obeyed laws which were so beautiful and so clear that all music seemed to speak of God. My body was not listening, it was praying. My spirit no longer had bounds, and if tears came to my eyes, I did not feel them running down because they were outside me. I wept with gratitude every time the orchestra began to sing.
> I love Mozart so much, I loved Beethoven so much that in the end they made me what I am. They molded my emotions and guided my thoughts. Is there anything in me which I did not, one day, receive from them? I doubt it. (pp. 92–3)

We shouldn't just listen. We should also sing. Jack Kornfield (1993) tells a wonderful story about a tribe in Africa that connects each child to a song. When the mother wants to conceive a child with her mate, she goes and sits under a tree until she can hear the song of the child she hopes to conceive. Once she hears the song she comes back to the village and shares with her husband. They sing the song while they make love, hoping the child hears them. When the baby starts to grow in the womb, the mother, along with other women in the village, sings the song to the baby. Throughout labor and during birth the baby is greeted by his or her song. Most of the village learns the song so that it can be sung to the child whenever he or she becomes hurt or is in danger. The song is also sung during various rituals in the child's life. For example, the song is sung when the person marries. When the person is on the death-bed, friends and relatives gather to sing the song for the last time.

Angeles Arrien states (1995) "When we go to a medicine person or healer because we are feeling disheartened or depressed, he or she might ask questions like, 'When did you stop singing? When did you stop dancing?'" (p. 175)

Soul Journal

It is helpful to have a place where we can write down our deepest feelings and longings. For example, we can write about our love and feelings for others here. We can record moments when we felt the ego drop away and the soul was exposed. Marion Woodman (1995) writes:

> Another way I nurture my soul is by keeping a daily journal. My journal is my soul book. It is my dialogue with God. Since the age of twelve, I have searched for my essence, and I have recorded my terrors, my hopes, my delights in my journal. In doing this I have affirmed my own feelings and my own values. I have sought to discover my unique purpose. In this way, I have tried to live my own truth, which often ran counter to the culture. (p. 34)

Every day Woodman spends two hours early in the morning meditating, visualizing, doing yoga, working on dreams, or writing in her journal.

Honoring Space and Silence

I believe that in North America, we fear silence and space. Most silences that we experience particularly with other people are uncomfortable so we fill in the spaces with chit-chat. If we are alone, we usually feel the need to have the radio or television on. We seem to need the noise, otherwise we would have to listen to our own thoughts.

We also seem to need to fill up physical space. Our houses are filled with stuff. As I mentioned earlier, our classrooms too can become cluttered with every wall covered with posters and student work. In the city, neon lights and billboards compete for our attention. In short, there is no balance between object and space. In the east, particularly in Japan there has long been a tradition of simplicity with regard to space. For example, there is little furniture as people simply sit on the floor. Asian art reflects this sense of space as often objects in paintings are small and surrounded by large amounts of space.

I respect the spirit of the Quaker meeting that is held in silence till someone is moved to speak and then he or she attempts to speak from the heart. *Faith and Practice* of New York Yearly Meeting puts it this way:

> We approach the meeting confidently, listening to the still small voice within . . . in active waiting, we strive to dissociate the mind from distractions and to focus inwardly. As each of us helps and strengthens others in this process, worship becomes a corporate experience. (p. 16)

Our culture is drowning in sound bites and chatter. The more we talk the less we hear.

Our education system too has little respect for silence. In silence, we can learn to listen to voices of the earth. We can also begin to hear other people at a much deeper level. Some schools have periods of silent reading where students can read anything they want. I think this is a valuable addition to the school day just for the silence alone.

By honoring silence and space, we begin to bring some sort of balance to our culture and our lives. With this balance we can develop a new rhythm between talk and silence, object and space. The Japanese call this space *ma*.

> Respect for *ma* deters us from plunging ahead when the right time for action is still impending. Gifted actors and comedians, great speakers and leaders, have an instinct for this quality. We have all noted the pause just prior to an important point when participants are momentarily waiting for release from tension created in part by the pause itself. But, as in theater, so also in organizational life, the magic fusion between anticipation and execution often fizzles. We have all witnessed a flow of organizational events building effectively toward closure only to see the overeager clumsily destroy consensus with a premature plunge toward the finish line. Such haste is as disastrous in organizations as in the theater. (Pascale and Athos 1981, p. 144)

By using various forms of meditation, slowing down, listening to music, honoring silence and space, we develop a contemplative approach to life and thus nurture the soul. Caring for the soul requires us to look at our lives and to make changes because the direction of modern life is so counter to the needs of the soul.

However, it is also important that we live life. Sometimes those who are attracted to contemplation and a more "spiritual life" use meditation and spiritual practices as a form of escape. Spirituality, then, is used as a defense mechanism. Matthew Fox's (1995) words are important here:

> There are no set rules for nourishing the soul, no "three steps to guaranteed soulfulness." Loving, laughing, crying, creating, praying, tilting with windmills, raising a child, saying good-bye to a departed loved one—it's all living, if we're aware of what we're doing. Some embrace life naturally; others have to learn. Some readily open themselves to life; others can only do so after a breakdown or calamity. For all of us, however, it is a question of living of being alive and aware of what's really going on. Living life is nourishing to the soul—and there's a lot of living to do. (p. 154)

James Wilkes, a psychiatrist with a theological background writes:

> When St. Paul writes, "Therefore my brothers and sisters, I implore you by God's mercy to offer your very selves to him: a living sacrifice dedicated and fit for his acceptance, the worship offered by mind and heart," (Romans 12:1) sacrifice no longer pertains only to concrete religious acts of sacrifice but to our living bodies and lives . . . his compelling word here is the word "living." The sacrifice is the living; it is the action of our lives. (pp. 48–49)

Living life fully is perhaps the most essential key to nurturing the soul; not running from the pain and suffering as well as embracing the natural joys of life. When love comes to your life, embrace it and rejoice. When there is parting through death or separation, grieve. And through it all be aware of what's happening to you and to your feelings.

Much of modern life is deadening. The mad rush, commercials, and sitcoms are our daily menu. We need to rescue our souls by living life fully. As John Cleese (Skynner and Cleese, 1993) said: "Mike Nichols told me that his brother, who is a doctor, says that he has never yet seen anyone on a deathbed who has confessed: 'I wish I'd spent more time at the office.'" (p. 318) Emerson said (1990) "The way of life is wonderful: it is by abandonment." (p. 200). By living with abandon we can begin the process of restoring soul.

Listen to the words of Nadine Stair who wrote this when she was eighty-five.

> If I had my life to live over.
>
> I'd like to make more mistakes next time. I'd relax. I would limber up. I would be sillier than I have been this trip. I would do fewer things seriously. I would take more chances. I would climb more mountains and swim more rivers. I would eat more ice cream and less beans. I would perhaps have more actual troubles, but I'd have fewer imaginary ones.
>
> You see, I'm one of those people who live sensibly and sanely hour after hour, day after day. Oh, I've had my moments, and if I had it to do over again, I'd have more of them. In fact I'd try to have nothing else. Just moments, one after another, instead of living so many years ahead of each day. I've been one of those persons who never goes anywhere without a thermometer, a hot water bottle, a raincoat, and a parachute. If I had to do it again, I would travel lighter than I have.
>
> If I had my life to live over, I would start barefoot earlier in the spring and stay that way later in the fall. I would go to more dances. I would ride more merry-go-rounds. I would pick more daisies. (Cited in Dass, p. 5)

FINAL THOUGHTS

This chapter is based on the assumption that some of the most important work we can do is on ourselves. How can we hope to help heal the planet unless we are willing to heal ourselves? Through contemplation we can nourish our own souls, which will in turn help create a positive environment for our children's souls. There is a connection between our inner and outer lives and in our culture and we have tended to ignore this relationship. By living contemplatively we can begin to create deep and powerful change in our world. In this next chapter I will explore how we can approach such change from a soulful perspective.

9

Change and the Soul

In this final chapter I will summarize the major themes of the book and explore how we can bring soul into our teaching and the life of the school.

PRINCIPLES OF SOULFUL LEARNING

1. *The sacred and secular cannot be separated.* Modern life is based on the secularization of life and the compartmentalization of the sacred. Yet most saints and mystics throughout the centuries have stated that separating the secular from the sacred is creating a false dichotomy because the two are inextricably intertwined. Mother Theresa, as I noted earlier, stated that she does small acts with great love; in other words, everything she did she saw as a spiritual act. Aung San Suu Kyi (1997), who won the Nobel Peace Prize for her work in Burma states: "Everywhere you'll find this drive to separate the secular from the spiritual. . . . I think some people find it embarassing and impractical to think of the spiritual and political life as one. I do not see them as separate" (p. 26). Referring to education Gandhi (1980) said:

> A proper and all round development of the mind, therefore, can take place only when it proceeds *pari passu* with the education of the physical and spiritual faculties of the child. They constitute an indivisible whole. According to this theory, therefore, it would be a gross fallacy to suppose that they can be developed piecemeal or independently of one another. (p. 189)

It is interesting that a Christian, Buddhist and Hindu all agree on how the sacred cannot be separated from the rest of life.

2. *The dominance of the secular has led to a repression of our spiritual life.* Here I would like to quote Warren Nord (1995) who has written an important book entitled *Religion and American Education.*

> We modern-day Americans have a spiritual problem. There is some-
> thing fundamentally wrong with our culture. We who have suc-
> ceeded so brilliantly in matters of economics, science, and technol-
> ogy have been less successful in matters of the heart and soul. This is
> evident in our manners and our morale: in our entertainment and
> our politics; in our preoccupation with sex and violence; in the ways
> we do our jobs and in the failure of our relationships; in our bore-
> dom and unhappiness in this, the richest of all societies. (p. 380)

Public education has, of course, been part of this process as it has
also been a principal element in secuarlization. I agree with Nord
and believe that the price we pay is the violence and alienation that
so many people in our society experience.

3. *An awareness of soul can restore a balance to our educational vision.*
Soul is defined in this book as a vital energy that can give purpose
and meaning to life. By reawakening to soul in our lives we can
bring a balance to our inner and outer lives.

What I have proposed in this book relates more to spirituality
than religion. Spirituality is not confined to institutional religion
but is concerned with the connection we can feel between ourselves
and something vast, unseen, mysterious, and wondrous. Because
the spiritual is not connected to a particular set of religious beliefs it
does not fit within some of the legal rulings on the separation
between church and state that have been applied to schools in the
United States. Because the spiritual can permeate every aspect of
life it is impossible to keep it out of the classroom. For example, if a
student feels a sense of awe and wonder while studying the history
of the universe, can this spiritual experience somehow be excluded? The same principle could apply to so many other events
that happen in school including listening to or playing music, reading poetry, listening to a story, playing a sport, or writing in one's
journal. Trying to exclude the spiritual from the classroom removes
one of the most important aspects of learning, which is this sense of
wonder that can arise when learning something new.

4. *We can nourish the student's soul through various curriculum approaches and teaching/learning strategies.* Some of the ways described
in this book include a curriculum for the inner life, use of the arts,
and earth education. Other means include service education where
students are involved in community projects. Some of these projects were outlined in chapter 7. Some suggestions that I have made
are controversial such as the use of meditation. Each teacher must

work with the techniques that he/she feels are most appropriate in his/her context. For example, in the United States the use of guided imagery has been opposed by Christian fundamentalists while in Canada there has been much less opposition. I mentioned that the use of meditation in schools is increasing in England. In my own work I have found that teachers in Catholic schools have been able to use almost all of the techniques suggested here without any problems. So each teacher must be the judge of what approach is most appropriate for the community within which he/she works.

5. *The authentic and caring presence of the teacher can nourish the student's soul.* Even if a teacher feels constrained using some of the suggestions made in this book, working on being an authentic presence to students is probably the most important means of nourishing soul. If students feel heard and affirmed in our presence this will support the development of their souls immeasurably. Being present in the way I am talking about requires effort and discipline. Eventually this discipline brings more of an effortless presence but effort is required in the beginning. Energy is required because our minds are pulled in so many different directions.

Compassion and caring also can contribute enormously to the nourishment of soul. Again the students must sense a genuine compassion coming from the teacher, the kind that Jessica Siegel was able to feel for her students after reading their autobiographies (chapter 4).

In the classroom where the teacher demonstrates authenticity, caring, thoughtfulness, and kindness, the student's soul can feel safe and more able to express itself.

6. *Soulful education must be accountable.* Teachers with a concern for soul have expectations that students will do well in their academic work as well as in their personal and spiritual growth. A soulful curriculum fully engages the student. I have not said much about assessment in this book. I believe much of the work on authentic assessment is helpful in providing evidence of how the student is doing. Communication between the teacher and parent is vital to the process of accountability. Ideally, parents who have continuous contact with the school and see what their children are doing day-to-day are the best form of accountability. Parents need to see what their children can actually do rather than reading a grade on a report card.

7. *Teachers need to nourish their own souls.* Teachers need to care for themselves, and various spiritual practices can provide much

needed energy and support. I have described many of these practices in chapter 8, which include approaching life more contemplatively. Every day we need to find some time where we allow
our mind and body to rest and I am not just referring to sleeping.
Some people call meditation a "coming home" because they find it
restful. For others gardening or walking can provide this rest and
nourishment for the soul.

Again making room for this time requires effort and discipline. It may mean getting up earlier in the morning or giving up
some television time.

8. *Parents can do much to nourish their childrens' souls.* Many of the
suggestions that I have made for teachers can be applied to parents.
First the parents need to be present and mindful. The child who
feels heard by his or her parents is the child who feels affirmed and
validated. How much of children's "acting out" is really a cry to be
heard?

The young child's soul can also be nourished through reading and telling fairy tales and stories. Fairy tales and stories can
often be rich in images that nourish the child's inner life. When
children are older encourage them to read myths and stories from
various religious and spiritual traditions. Of course, as parents we
need to model the behavior we want our children to engage in so
that they can see that reading spiritually significant literature is also
important to us.

Take children for walks in nature. The earth activities described in chapter 6 can be used by parents to introduce children to
the wonders of nature. Place flowers in your house and start a
garden; encourage your children to look after their own plant (s).

Be aware of the aesethetic and musical evironment of the
home. Is it pleasing and nourishing? Provide materials for the
young child to draw and paint.

SPIRITUALITY, SOUL, AND RELIGION

I have argued in this book that spiritual experience is not limited to
religious experience but can occur outside a religious context. Of
course, it can also occur within religion.

Nord (1995) makes a very strong case for making the study of
religion compulsory at the secondary and undergraduate levels. He
argues that in our secular education system we have excluded almost all discussion of religion. He suggests that our young people
are illiterate when it comes to their knowledge of religious matters.

I agree with much of the argument that Nord presents. I also believe that spirituality and soul should also be examined in relation, but not limited to, the various religions. I have argued in other contexts (Miller 1996) that students in secondary school should have the opportunity to study the world religions. Like Nord, I believe that religion is an integral part of many cultures and in fact is at the heart of many cultures such as cultures in the Middle East. I also believe that students should have the opportunity to read from the memoirs of various religious figures to get a sense of the variety of spiritual experiences within a religious context. For example, in another context I (1994) have described spiritual lives of the Buddha, Gandhi, St. Theresa of Avila, and Thomas Merton.

Nord states:

> Just as racially segregated schools are inherenty unequal, so an exclusively secular education is inherently not neutral. Religious and secular ways of understanding the world must be taught together; schools and universities must be religiously integrated. . . .
>
> The curriculum must provide students with the intellectual, imaginative, and emotional resources to understand religion from the "inside," empathetically, and allow religious ideas and values to contend with secular ideas and values for the informed, critical judgment of students. (pp. 378–79)

I would add that schools and universities must also be spiritually integrated. Integrating spirituality into the life of the school means simply aknowledging that students have an inner life that needs nourishment

SOULFUL CHANGE

How can we bring about some of the changes suggested in this book? I believe that much of the literature on educational change is written from the secularist stance that is inadequate in addressing how to bring soul into our schools and classrooms. As an alternative to this literature I would like to briefly present a model developed by Parker Palmer and then discuss some basic principles of soulful change.

Parker Palmer's Model of Change

Parker Palmer has written extensively about spirituality in education and in his latest book, *The Courage to Teach,* he provides a model that I feel is congruent with this book. Palmer develops his approach based on what he calls a "movement mentality" that is drawn from movements like the civil rights movement or the women's movement. There are four stages to the model:

> *Stage 1.* Isolated individuals make an inward decision to live "*divided no more,*" finding a center for their lives outside of institutions.
>
> *Stage 2.* These individuals begin to discover one another and form *communities of congruence* that offer mutual support and opportunities to develop a shared vision.
>
> *Stage 3.* These communities start *going public,* learning to convert their private concerns into the public issues and they are receiving vital critiques in the process.
>
> *Stage 4.* A system of *alternative rewards* emerges to sustain the movement's vision and to put pressure for change on the standard institutional reward system. (p. 166)

1. *The Undivided Life.* The first stage involves finding an undivided center within so that one's soul is not controlled by the institution. The example that Palmer cites is Rosa Parks who refused to give up her seat on the bus in Montgomery Alabama. This act ignited much of the civil rights movement. Parks came to the point where she could no longer submit to the institution of racism and had found the strength within herself to act accordingly. At this point the person realizes the institution will only change if the he or she takes some action based on this undivided self. The undivided life could also be called the "soulful life" as the person now lives congruently with his or her soul.

Palmer has found that the teachers he meets across the United States are starting to live the undivided, or soulful life. He finds that these teachers "affirm their deep caring for the lives of students, and they do not want to disconnect from the young. They understand the identity and integrity that they have invested in teaching, and they want to reinvest, even if it pays no institutional interest or dividends" (p. 171). Palmer also states that teachers are willing to challenge institutional constraints and argue for alternative visions of education.

Like Rosa Parks these teachers are willing to take risks because they feel that they can no longer work under conditions that they feel are counter to almost everything that they believe in as teachers.

2. *Communities of Congruence.* In the second stage people who have committed to the undivided life begin to come together into com-

munities of congruence. These communities offer mutual support for their beliefs and actions. They also help people develop a language that is representative of the movement's vision. Palmer suggests this is often a language of the heart that at first sounds fragile because it is rarely used in mainstream society. The communities also encourage people to learn and try skills that they need to make the changes that they are committed to.

Palmer believes that the black churches were the communities of congruence for the civil rights movement. In education he refers to different networks and associations that are supporting change. I am a member of the Association of Supervision and Curriculum Development and within that Association there are about fifty networks including one for Holistic Learning and Spirituality in Education where educators can come together to share their concerns and hopes for change. These networks are allowing people to explore and express their views. Palmer encourages people to publicly declare their vision and he says: "when we declare our values in a visible and viable way, we will sometimes be amazed at the way allies gather around" (p. 175).

3. *Going Public.* By making the movement public the people involved can avoid the difficulty of becoming too insular. By going public the movement opens itself to public criticism. Also it allows the movement to broaden its base and make connections with people in other fields such as business, medicine, and government. Palmer notes that nontraditional teaching approaches have already found their way into business. The challenge of going public can lead to real growth within the movement:

> As a movement goes public, the identity and integrity of its participants are tested against the great diversity of values and visions at work in the public arena. We must stay close to our own integrity in this complex field of forces, where we can easily lose our way. But we must also risk opening ourselves to conflicting influences, for in that way both the movement and our integrity can grow. (p. 179)

4. *The Heart's Reward.* The changes that a movement can bring are often modest. They lead not to radical reform by alterations within institutions; yet even small changes can now allow people committed to change to grow and prosper within the institution. For example, in my own institution, The Ontario Institute for Studies in Education at the University of Toronto, we have formed a unit within my department called Holistic and Aesthetic Education

where faculty and students feel comfortable addressing issues of spirituality. I now teach a course on spirituality in education. I was also pleased to learn this year that there is a Holistic Teaching/Learning Unit at the University of Tennessee. Of course, the label "holistic" does not guarantee authentic change but it can allow for more experimentation and more open discussion to alternative approaches in teaching and learning. By recognizing areas such as holistic education or transformational education, universities and colleges can do much to legitimize alternative visions of learning.

The main reward comes from knowing that you have been true to your own integrity and thus have had real impact on the students you teach.

> If you are here faithfully with us, you are bringing abundant blessing. It is a blessing known to generations of students whose lives have been transformed by people who had the courage to teach—the courage to teach from the most truthful places in the landscape of self and world, the courage to invite students to discover, explore, and inhabit those places in the living of their own lives. (p. 183)

The soul feels the rewards of this kind of approach to change and it senses that it's destiny is being fulfilled rather than repressed or thwarted.

Taoist Change

Approaches to change generally reflect a linear view of reality that have been based on implementing educational innovations in a rational, systematic manner. In general, these approaches haven't worked because they lack a broader, more comprehensive view of change and reality itself. As an alternative, I believe that one of the best conceptions of change comes from Taoism. We are familiar with the Taoist symbol of the ying/yang yet there remains, I believe, a basic lack of understanding about the larger reality that underlies this diagram (Fig. 9.1). I would like to describe the essential elements of Taoist change and then apply them to change that would be conducive to bringing soul into education.

Balance. From the Taoist view the Universe is dynamically balanced between opposite polarities: masculine/feminine; light/dark; active/passive; inner/outer; rational/intuitive. Each polarity, however, contains the seed of its opposite as the two polarities need each other to exist. This is an important element in understanding

Fig. 9.1 Yin/Yang Symbol

the nature of change. I have argued elsewhere (Miller 1994, 1996) that the yang qualities have dominated in the West for the past several hundred years to the exclusion of the yin qualities. This imbalance I believe has led to illness within the Western world that we see in the violence and lack of spiritual awareness we find in our culture. I believe that the women's movement and the recent interest in spirituality is an attempt to restore a dynamic balance to our culture. In education too we need to restore a balance between elements such as content/process, individual learning/group learning, learning/assessment, technology/program, basic skill learning/creative learning. In general, we tend to emphasize one form of learning over its polarity and again this leads to imbalance in our schools. As I noted earlier, an emphasis on soul needs to balance our emphasis on the traditional curriculum that has ignored the student's inner life.

Also as teachers and educational leaders we need to find balance within ourselves. First, our lives need to be balanced between our work and our personal lives, a balance that many people today find difficult to achieve. Second, we need to find an inner balance between ying/yang qualities within ourselves. When we are able to create this inner balance we feel energetic and can experience what Csikszentmihalyi (1988) calls the "flow experience." In the flow experience we find ourselves deeply in touch with what we are doing.

The concept of balance can help us avoid unnecessary conflict in educational change. In terms of bringing soul into our work it helps us realize that we need to keep an awareness of the "outer curriculum" and not try to focus the curriculum solely on the inner life of the student. Ideally, we want to create a dynamic *rhythm* in our classrooms between the polarities. When this rhythm exists, it leads to student engagement in learning and the flow experience.

Finally, we should realize the balance can be something very simple and natural:

> Balance is not an unusual experience, not some esoteric device that is available only to the exceptionally self-disciplined or the diligent followers of the Way. It is common and unavoidable. Everyone has it and practices it. It is the inner condition that moves each person from one day to the next that surmounts momentary frustration and deep trauma. It is the composure that instills patience, the calm that solves problems, the natural urge that inspires healing. (Grigg 1994, p. 256)

Paradox. Closely related to the concept of balance is that of paradox since as we hold the opposites in balance we create a paradoxical tension. As R. H. Blyth (1976) has stated: "We have to live between the relative and absolute, in both at the same time" (p. 162) Living between the masculine and feminine, rational and intuitive, active and passive at the same time creates paradox that can sometimes cause deep confusion because the paradox cannot be solved through logic. Instead, it requires some sort of leap to embrace the paradox from a larger perspective.

As I noted in my explanation of the nature of soul in chapter 2, the soul tends to be more comfortable with paradox than with rational thought. It can embrace the opposites and this embrace can sometimes lead to a synthesis of ideas.

In change we are often faced with many paradoxes. One of the most often quoted is that "the more things change the more they stay the same." Another paradoxical tension we hear often is the polarity between whole language and phonics. If teachers and leaders in the school can embrace the paradoxes that arise they may attain some sort of synthesis that allows us to move forward rather than being overwhelmed by the paradoxes that confront us. For example, the supposed tension between the two approaches to language does not have to be an "either/or" choice but a synthesis of both.

Wordlessness. We are overwhelmed by the spoken and written word, yet much change occurs silently within the soul of the person and the soul of the institution. However, our lack of sensitivity to the nonverbal means that we often overlook elements that contribute to successful change within an institution. The problem with words is that they can never totally convey the meaning of direct experience.

It is the manner and presence of the leader that can have as much to do with how change occurs within the school as what he or she says. The nature of eye contact, for example, is one of those subtle and sometimes not so subtle factors that can affect relationships within the school. Also the tone of our speech can have as much impact as what we say. If we can be more aware of the nonverbal there is a tendency for a spaciousness to develop within our classrooms and schools that allows teachers and students to feel more at home. Again the spaces between what we say allow our words to have meaning. If we crowd these spaces, our speech tends to lose its impact.

Emerson (1990) noted with regard to the soul, "The action of the soul is oftener in that which is felt and left unsaid , then that which is said" (p. 178). So it is often in the silent spaces that the soul can see what needs to be done.

Selflessness. Selflessness does not refer to a denial of self but placing our sense of self within a larger context. In the West we tend to look at the self as something hard and fixed. This rigidity can also make change vary difficult as we begin to over identify with our sense of self and this over identification can lead to inflexibility. However, if we can soften the edges around the sense of self we can learn to identify with others and see their point of view. Change can become much more organic if we see our self within a larger context of being. Grigg (1994) describes the possible results of this awareness:

> A profound compassion for everything is accompanied by a corresponding sense that each individual part of wholeness has it own course that belongs to the integrated pattern of everything. All details have context. And this deep awareness of context permits each person to move harmoniously within the moment-by-moment unfolding of a great wisdom. (p. 209)

In the context of this book by loosening our sense of self we can attune to another person's soul and recognize that the soul has its own unique role to play within the school. Recognizing the uniqueness of each soul within the school staff may allow "each person to move harmoniously" within the school's overall context and contribute to a deeper unfolding within the school. Again many of the suggestions made in the last chapter can assist in this process.

When we loosen boundaries of self we can then find that some larger energy works through us. Emerson (1990) wrote:

> Standing on the bare ground, my head bathed by the blithe air and uplifted into infinite space,-all mean egotism vanishes. I become a transparent eyeball, I am nothing, I see all, the currents of the Universal Being circulate through me, I am part and particle of God. (p. 18)

Here our action becomes the optimum action. Below is the story of how a cook learned to cut the oxen without self.

> Prince Wen Hui remarked, "How wonderfully you have mastered your art."
>
> The cook laid down his knife and said, "What your servant really cares for is Tao, which is beyond mere art. When I first began to cut up oxen, I saw nothing but oxen. After three years of practicing, I no longer saw the ox as a whole. I now work with my spirit, not with my eyes. My senses stop functioning and my spirit takes over. (Feng and English 1974, p. 55)

Like the cook, I believe that our best teaching occurs when our spirit and soul take over.

Softness/Spontaneity. People in the East talk about individuals having the quality of softness that should be balanced with hardness within the person. In the West with our masculine emphasis we have tended to value hardness particularly in men. Yet the "hardness" in a man or women can be a huge barrier to change. Franck (1978) notes this problem that goes back to the Greeks:

> The Greeks could not for a moment give up their heads, their rational questions and rational answers. The Chinese, if it is not too rude to say so, had no heads from the beginning, and the same may be said of the Japanese, who have always hated logic and psychology, and perhaps always will. The Greeks were men, and the Chinese and Japanese were women, and women are always more right than men. (pp. 13–4)

"Women" tend to be more right because of this softness, which means "being embracing and fluid, inclusive, and flexible" (Grigg p. 215). When we soften we also allow ourselves to be more spontaneous. The qualities of softness and spontaneity are often compared to images in nature, particularly water. So the spontaneity that arises is not a random spontaneity but in accord with nature. Emerson (1990) wrote:

> All good conversation, manners, and action, come from a spontaneity which forgets usages and makes the moment great. Nature hates calculators; her methods are saltatory and impulsive. . . . For practical success there must not be too much design. (pp. 237–38)

I would add to Emerson's list of "conversation, manners, and action" education, which has often been forced into rigid models including one of the most recent—outcome-based education— where there is little opportunity for spontaneous action. Again there should be a balance between planned action and the spontaneous.

The soul thrives in a climate where spontaneity is present and it withers in an environment that is overplanned and controlled. In education we have given room for the spontaneous when we talk of the "teachable moment." For schools there are also teachable moments with regard to change where school leaders find the opportunity arises to try something different. Here the teacher, or school leader, through his or her intuition senses that people in that moment are ready to try something new.

According to the Tao change is the way of nature. By attuning ourselves to this way we can begin to align ourselves with change rather than trying to control or impose our will on it. At an institutional level through such factors as balance, silence, paradox, self-lessness, and spontaneity we can begin to create conditions where change unfolds organically rather than through some contrived model. This does not mean that there will not be confusion and conflict but instead we can address the difficulties from a more balanced and spacious perspective. The soul becomes an essential element in this process. It thrives in an atmosphere of paradox, silence, and spontaneity and thus can contribute to the change that is unfolding. In this type of environment the soul can sense what is needed at the right moment and contributes in a positive manner to the changes that are occurring in the school.

References

Arrien, Angeles (1995). "Gateway to the Soul." In *Handbook for the Soul*, edited by Richard Carlson and Benjamin Shield. Boston: Little, Brown & Co.

Aung San Suu Kyi, and Clements, Alan (1997). *The Voice of Hope*. New York: Seven Stories Press.

Barrett, William (1962). *Irrational Man: A Study in Existential Philosophy*. New York: Doubleday Anchor.

Bastian, L. (1987). "Learning from Your Dreams." *Youth Update*. Cincinnati: St. Anthony Messenger Press.

Benson, Herbert (1976). *The Relaxation Response*. New York: Avon.

Bliss, Hope C. (1992). "Creating Value in the Hoikuen." *Holistic Education Review* 5:52–57.

Bloom, Alan (1993). *Love and Friendship*. New York: Simon & Schuster.

Blyth, Robert (1976). In *Games Zen Masters Play: Writings of R. H. Blyth*. Robert Sohl and Audrey Carr (eds.) New York: Mentor.

Borysenko, Joan (1993). *Fire in the Soul*. New York: Warner Books.

——— (1995). "Ensouling Ourselves." In *Handbook for the Soul*. Edited by Richard Carlson and Benjamin Shield. Boston: Little, Brown.

Campbell, P. S., and Scott-Kassner, C. (1995). *Music in Childhood: From Preschool through the Elementary Grades*. New York: Schirmer Books.

Capadli, N.; Kelly, E.; and Navia, L. (1981). *An Invitation to Philosophy*. New York: Prometheus.

Carrington, Patricia (1977). *Freedom in Mediation*. New York: Doubleday.

Chase, Margaret Portney (1974). *Just Being at the Piano*. Berkeley, Calif.: Creative Arts Books.

Christie, L. (1983). *"Writers and Dreamers: An Exploratory Study of Ninth-grade English Students."* Doctoral dissertation, the University of North Dakota. Dissertation Abstracts International, ACC 8404854.

Clark, Frances (1975). "Fantasy and Imagination." In *Four Psychologies Applied to Education*, edited by T. B. Roberts, pp. 498–513. New York: John Wiley & Sons.

Corcoran, Peter, and Horne, Eric (1996). "The Soul in Soule School." *Holistic Education Review* 9:24–28.

Covey, Stephen (1990). *The Seven Habits of Highly Effective People.* New York: Simon & Schuster.

Crisp, Terry (1990). *Dream Dictionary.* New York: Dell Publishing.

Csikszentmihalyi, M., & Csikszentmihalyi, I. S. eds. (1988). *Optimal Experience: Psychological Studies of Flow in Consciousness.* Cambridge: Cambridge University Press.

Dalai Lama (1994). *A Flash of Lightning in the Dark of Night: A Guide to the Bodhisattva's Way of Life.* Boston: Shambhala.

Dalla Costa, John (1995). *Working Wisdom: The Ultimate value in the New Economy.* Toronto: Stoddart.

Dass, Ram (1978). *Journey of Awakening: A Meditator's Guidebook.* New York: Bantam.

de Nicholas, Antonio (1989). *Habits of Mind: An Introduction to the Philosophy of Education.* New York: Paragon.

Dee, Nerys (1984). *Your Dreams and What They Mean: How to Understand the Secret Language of Sleep.* Hammersmith, U.K.: The Aquarian Press.

Doll, M. (1982). "Beyond the Window: Dreams and Learning." *Journal of Curriculum Theorizing,* 4.1: 197–201.

Elkind, David (1981). *The Hurried Child: Growing Up Too Fast Too Soon.* Reading, Mass.: Addison Wesley.

Emerson, Ralph Waldo (1990). *Ralph Waldo Emerson: Selected Essays, Lectures, and Poems.* Edited by R. D. Richardson Jr. New York. Bantam.

Fassel, Diane (1990). *Working Ourselves to Death.* San Francisco: HarperSanFrancisco.

Feng, Gia, and English, Jane, trans. (1974). *Chang Tzu: Inner Chapters.* New York: Vintage.

Fox, Matthew (1988). *The Coming of the Cosmic Christ.* San Francisco: HarperSanFrancisco.

Fox, Matthew (1994). *The Reinvention of Work: A New Vision of Livelihood for Our Time.* San Francisco: HarperCollins.

Fox, Matthew (1995). "Soul Creation" in *Handbook for the Soul* Richard Carlson and Benjamin Shield (eds). Boston: Little, Brown.

Franck, Frederick (1978). *Zen and Zen Classics.* New York: Vintage.

Freedman, Samuel (1990). *Small Victories: The Real World of a Teacher, Her Students and Their High School.* New York: Harper & Row.

Gandhi, Mohandas (1980). *All Men Are Brothers: Autobiographical Reflections.* Krishna Kripalani, ed. New York: Continuum.

Gaylean, Beverly-Collene (1983). *Mindsight: Learning through Imaging.* Healdsburg, Calif.: Center for Integrative Learning.

Geldard, Richard (1993). *The Esoteric Emerson: The Spiritual Teachings of Ralph Waldo Emerson.* Hudson, N.Y.: Lindisfarne Press.

Goethe, Johann von (1970). *Theory of Colors*. Cambridge: MIT Press.

Goldberg, Merryl (1997). *Arts and Learning: An Integrated Approach to Teaching and Learning in Multicultural and Multilingual Settings*. New York: Longman.

Goldstein, Joseph (1975). *The Experience of Insight*. Boston:Shambhala

Goleman, Daniel (1995). *Emotional Intelligence: Why It Can Matter More Than IQ*. New York: Bantam.

Gore, Al (1992). *Earth in the Balance: Ecology and the Human Spirit*. Boston: Houghton Mifflin.

Grallert, Margot (1991). "Working from Inside Out: A Practical Approach to Expression." *Harvard Educational Review* 61. 3.

Grigg, Ray (1994). *The Tao of Zen*. Boston: Charles E. Tuttle.

Grumet, Madeline (1988). *"The Child's Dream Narrative and the Curriculum."* Doctoral dissertation, the University of Rochester. Dissertation Abstracts International, ACC 8806607.

Hancock, L. with Rosenberg, D.; Springen, K.; King, P.; Rogers, P; Brant, M.; Kalb, C.; Gegax, T. (1995). "Breaking Point." *Newsweek,* March 6, 1995, pp. 56–61.

Hanh, Tich Nat (1976). *The Miracle of Mindfulness! A manual on meditation*. Boston: Beacon Press.

——— (1991). *Peace is Every Step: The Path of Mindfulness in Everyday Life*. New York: Bantam.

Hawley, Jack (1993). *Reawakening the Spirit in Work*. New York: Simon & Schuster.

Hayes, Rosemary (1975). "Do You Have Your Dream for English?" In *Four Psychologies Applied to Education* edited by T. B. Roberts, pp. 417–20. New York: John Wiley & Sons.

Heschel, A. J. (1951). *The Sabbath*. New York: Farrar, Straus & Giroux.

Hillman, James (1996). *The Soul's Code: In Search of Character and Calling*. New York: Random House.

Hoffman, E. (1980). "The Kabbalah." *The Journal of Humanistic Psychology*. 20:33–47.

Holmes, Oliver W. (1885, 1980). *Ralph Waldo Emerson*. Boston: Houghton Mifflin.

Holt, John (1991). *Never Too Late*. New York. Toronto: Addison-Wesley. (Original work published 1978.)

Hunt, David E. (1987). *Beginning with Ourselves: In Practice, Theory, and Human Affairs*. Toronto: OISE Press.

——— (1992). *Renewing Personal Energy*. Toronto: OISE Press.

James, Jamie (1993). *The Music of the Spheres: Music, Science, and the Natural Order of the Universe*. New York: Grove Press.

Jones, Howard Mumford, ed. (1996). *Emerson on Education*. New York: Teachers College Press.

Jung, Carl J. (1974). *Dreams.* Princeton, N. J.: Princeton University Press.

Kabat-Zinn, Jon (1990). *Full Catastrophe Living: Using the Wisdom of Your Body and Mind to Face Sress, Pain, and Illness.* New York: Delacorte Press.

Kessler, R., and Larsen L. (1994). Community Arts and Education Partnership: Toward a Comprehensive Arts and Education Program for Metropolitan Toronto through Community Partnerships. Toronto. Royal Conservatory of Music.

Kincher, J. (1988). *Dreams Can Help a Journal Guide to Understanding Your Dreams and Making Them Work for You.* Minneapolis: Free Spirit Publishing.

Kohn, Alfie (1993). *Punished by Rewards: The Trouble with Gold Stars, Incentive Plans, A's Praise, and Other Bribes.* Boston: Houghton Mifflin.

Kornfield, Jack (1993). *A Path with Heart.* New York: Bantam.

Lara, Adair (1994). *Slowing Down in a Speeded Up World.* Berkeley, Calif.: Conari Press.

Layton, B., trans. (1987). *The Gnostic Scriptures.* London: SCM Press Ltd.

LeShan, Lawrence (1974). *How to Meditate.* Boston: Little, Brown & Co.

Levete, Gina (1995). *Presenting the Case for Meditation in Primary and Secondary Schools. London:* The Interlink Trust.

Lopate, Phillip (1975). *Being with Children.* New York: Bantam.

Lusseyran, Jacques (1987). *And There was light.* New York: Parabola.

Macrorie, Karen (1984). *Twenty Teachers.* New York: Oxford University Press.

Makiguchi, T. (1989). *Education for Creative Living: Ideas and proposals of Tsunesuburo Makiguhi,* D. M. Bethel (ed.) Ames, IA: Iowa State University.

Mandela, Nelson (1994). *Long Walk to Freedom.* Boston: Little, Brown.

Matt, Daniel C. (1995). *The Essential Kabbalah: The Heart of Jewish Mysticism.* San Francisco: HarperSanFrancisco.

McLuhan, T. C. (1972). *Touch the Earth: A Self-Portrait of Indian Existence.* New York: Pocket Books.

Merton, Thomas (1959). "The Inner Experience. " Unpublished (four drafts at Thomas Merton Studies Center, Louisville, Ky.).

Miller, Jack (1995). "Meditating Teachers." *Inquiring Mind* 12:19–22.

Miller, John (1993). *The Holistic Teacher.* Toronto: OISE Press.

——— (1994). *The Contemplative Practitioner: Meditation in Education and the Professions.* Westport Conn.: Bergin and Garvey.

——— (1996). *The Holistic Curriculum.* Toronto: OISE Press.

Miller, Michael (1995). *Initimate Terrorism: The Deterioration of Erotic Life.* New York: W. W. Norton.

Moffett, James (1994). *The Universal Schoolhouse: Spiritual Awakening through Education.* San Francisco: Jossey-Bass.

Moore, Thomas (1992). *The Care of the Soul: A Guide for Cultivating Depth and Sacredness in Everyday Life.* New York: Walker (large print edition).

—— (1994). *SoulMates: Honoring the Mysteries of Love and Relationship.* New York: Harper.

Murdock, Maureen (1982). *Spinning Inward: Using Guided Imagery with Children.* Culver City, Calif.: Peace Press.

Murdoch, Iris (1992). *Metaphysics as a Guide to Morals.* London: Chatto & Windus.

Murray, Terry (1993). "The Black Rock Forest Project: Creating Connections in the Living Laboratory." *The Holistic Education Review* 6:44–55.

Neville, Bernie (1989). *Educating Psyche: Emotion, Imagination, and the Unconscious in Learning.* Victoria, Australia: Collins Dove.

New York Yearly Meeting (1995). *Faith and Practice.* New York: Author Press.

Noddings, Nel (1984). *Caring: A Feminine Approach to Ethics and Moral Education.* Berkeley: University of California Press.

Nord, Warren A. (1995). *Religion and American Education: Rethinking A National Dilemma.* Chapel Hill: University of North Carolina Press.

Orr, David W. (1994). *Earth in Mind: On Education, Environment and the Human Prospect.* Washington, D.C.: Island Press.

Pagels, E. (1989). *The Gnostic Gospels.* New York: Vintage-Random.

Palmer, Parker (1998). *The Courage to Teach: Exploring the Inner Landscape of a Teacher's Life.* San Francisco: Jossey-Bass.

Pascale, R. T., and Athos, A. G. (1981). *The Art of Japanese Management.* New York: Warner.

Paz, Octavio (1995). *The Double Flame: Love and Eroticism.* New York: Harcourt Brace.

Peters, F. E. (1982). *Children of Abraham.* Princeton, N.J.: Princeton University Press.

Polyani, Michael (1962). *Personal Knowledge: Towards a Post-Critical Philosophy.* Chicago: University of Chicago Press.

Quattrocchi, Marina (1994). *"What Are the Reactions, Revelations, and Repercussions of Dreamwork with Senior Sudents?"* Toronto: Unpublished paper.

—— (1995). *"Dreamwork in Secondary Schools: Its Educational Value and Personal Significance."* Doctoral dissertation, University of Toronto.

Reid, Sandra (1990). "Why Teach Singing Games? Part I" *Alla Brev* 15:13, 16–18.

—— (1991). "Why Teach Singing Games? Part II" *Alla Brev* 15:12–17.

—— (1995). "Why Teach Music?" *Federation of Women Teachers Association* 13:12–13.

—— (in press). "The Validity of Kodaly in Today's Changing Education." *Parlando: Hungarian Journal of Music Teachers Association.*

Richards, Mary Caroline (1980). *Toward Wholeness: Rudolf Steiner Education in America.* Middletown, Conn.: Wesleyan University.

Roberts, Elizabeth, and Amidon, Elias (1991). *Earth Prayers from around the World: 365 Prayers, Poems, and Invocations for Honoring the Earth.* New York: HarperCollins.

Robinson, Floyd (1998). Personal correspondence.

Roszak, Theodore (1992). *The Voice of the Earth.* New York: Simon & Schuster.

Rozman, Deborah (1976). *Mediation for Children.* Millbrae, California: Celestial Arts.

Sagarin, Stephen (1992). "Art in a Waldorf School." *Holistic Education Review* 5:19–24.

Salzberg, Sharon (1995). *Lovingkindness: The Revolutionary Art of Happiness.* Boston: Shambhala.

Samuels, Michael, and Samuels, Nancy (1975). *Seeing with the Mind's Eye.* New York: Random House Bookworks.

Sanford, J. A. (1968). *Dreams: God's Forgotten Language.* New York: Harper-Collins.

Sardello, Robert (1992). *Facing the World with Soul.* Hudson, N.Y.: Lindisfarne Press.

Sardello, Robert (1995). *Love and the Soul: Creating a Future for Earth.* New York: HarperCollins.

Saul, John R. (1995). *The Unconscious Civilization.* Concord, Ontario: Anansi Press.

Schon, Donald A. (1983). *The Reflective Practitioner: How Professionals Think in Action.* New York: Basic Books.

Secretan, Lance H. K. (1996). *Reclaiming Higher Ground: Creating Organizations That Inspire Soul.* Toronto: Macmillan.

Seed, John, and Macy, Joanna et al. (1988). *Thinking Like a Mountain.* Philadelphia: New Society Publishers.

Senge, Peter M. (1990). *The Fifth Discipline: The Art & Practice of the Learning Organization.* New York: Doubleday.

Shah, I. (1977, 1964). *The Sufis.* Suffolk, England. Chaucer Books. London. Star-W. H. Allen.

Singer, Jerome (1976). "Fantasy: The Foundation of Serenity." *Psychology Today,* July.

Skynner, Robin, and Cleese, John (1993). *Life and How to Survive It.* Markham, Ont.: Reed Books.

Smith, Huston (1986). *The Religions of Man.* New York: Harper.

——— (1994). *The Illustrated World's Religions.* San Francisco: HarperSanFrancisco.

Swimme, Brian, and Berry, Thomas (1992). *The Universe Story: From the Primordial Flaring Forth to Ecozoic Era. A Celebration of the Unfolding of the Cosmos.* San Francisco: Harper.

Terkel, Studs (1985). *Working.* New York: Ballantine.

Tezuka, Ikue (1995). *School with Forest and Meadow.* San Francisco: Caddo Gap Press.

Ullman, Montage, and Zimmerman, N. (1979). *Working with Dreams: Self-Understanding, Problem-Solving, and Enriched Creativity through Dream Appreciation.* Los Angeles: Jeremy P. Tarcher.

Wallis, Jim (1994). *The Soul of Politics.* New York: New Press.

Whyte, David (1994). *The Heart Aroused: Poetry and the Preservation of the Soul in Corporate America.* New York: Doubleday.

Wilber, K. (1995). *Spirituality, Sex and Ecology* Boston: Shambhala.

Wilkes, James R. (1993). *To Wrestle and to Dance: Reflections on the Power of Faith.* Toronto, Ont.: Viking Books.

Williams, Dilafruz; Taylor, Sarah; and Richter, John (1996). "Down-to-Earth Imagination and Soul-Nourishing Practices at the Environmental Middle School." *Holistic Education Review* 9:18–23.

Williams, Redford (1989) *The Trusting Heart: Great News about Behavior.* New York: Times Books.

Williamson, Marianne (1994). *Illuminata: Thought, Prayers, Rites of Passage.* New York: Random House.

Wilson, Colin (1985). *Rudolf Steiner: The Man and His Vision.* Wellingborough, U.K.: Aquarian Press.

Wolf, Fred A. (1996). *The Spiritual Universe: How Quantum Physics Proves the Existence of the Soul.* New York: Simon & Schuster.

Wood, G. H. (1992). *Schools That Work.* New York: Plume.

Woodman, Marion (1995). "Soul Moments." In *Handbook for the Soul,* edited by R. Carlson and B. Shield. Boston: Little, Brown & Co.

Index